MW00812581

STENNIS

Plowing a Straight Furrow

THE STORY OF STATESMAN JOHN C. STENNIS
By Don H. Thompson

For information contact Triton Press, 426 South Lamar Blvd., Suite 16, Oxford, MS 38655.

ISBN: 978-1-936-946-45-7 (limited edition hardcover)
ISBN: 978-1-936-946-46-4 (paperback)
ISBN: 978-1-936-946-47-1 (ebook)

Triton Press
A division of The Nautilus Publishing Company
426 South Lamar Blvd., Suite 16
Oxford, Mississippi 38655
Tel: 662-513-0159
www.nautiluspublishing.com
www.neilspector.com

First Edition

Front cover design by Connor Covert.
Front cover illustrations by Associated Press, courtesy of the Congressional and Political Research Center, Mississippi State University Libraries

A special thanks to the Stennis family for their support

Library of Congress Cataloging-in-Publication Data has been applied for
Printed in the United States of America

10 9 8 7 6 5 4 3 2 1

To my wife Rita

John C. Stennis taking the
Senate Oath of Office
in 1947

CONTENTS

*Stennis (second from left) began his formal education in a one-room school.
Photo courtesy of Margaret Stennis Womble.*

CHAPTER I
THE EARLY YEARS

"Growing Up in DeKalb"

DeKalb was not unlike most small Mississippi towns at the beginning of the twentieth century. The moneyed as well as the moneyless, along with the power brokers and the wannabes, the educated and those who could only make a mark, the good and the bad, all blended into what is a place.

For some, Kemper County was all they needed. Why would anyone want to venture any farther? But, given the right circumstances a few would. Maybe an athlete who made the majors or a hero from a faraway battlefield would find their names on a city limits' sign. But few could boast about one of their own who would become a confidant of presidents, an icon in Congress, and a benefactor to Mississippians long after his time. He would converse with foreign potentates and common folk as well, all the time comparing them and their lives to the only place he revered, Kemper County, Mississippi. It is interesting to see how this place and its people shaped the life of John Cornelius Stennis. From this small town in the Mississippi hills, he became "Mississippi's Statesman of the Century."

John Cornelius Stennis's formal education began in a one-room school established in 1903 in the Kipling community. Most one-room schoolhouses in the area were very rudimentary—a pot belly stove in the middle of the room, with benches surrounding it. The Stennis children walked two miles each day to attend classes. Accompanied to the small schoolhouse by his father on his first day, his initial lesson made quite an impression. His father warned him that if there were a problem, he and his mother would be on the teacher's side. Though shocking to the boy, this small lesson taught him respect for authority and the law, a lesson remaining with him throughout his life and career. The moral guidance he received at home, at church, and at school firmly set the foundations of integrity that would guide him for the rest of his life.

John Cornelius Stennis was born to Cornelia and Hampton Stennis on August 3, 1901, in the Kipling community south of DeKalb, Mississippi. Called "Mr. Hamp" by the locals, Stennis's father owned a couple of hundred acres of land. He was also associated with S. D. Stennis and Company, a mercantile business in DeKalb, owned by his brother, Dr. Samuel Adam Deberry Stennis. According to a neighbor, Mr. Hamp was devout, "never smoked or drank, or [did] anything [wrong]."[1] Quiet and unobtrusive in his daily walks, he was kind and thoughtful of others, one in whom you could place the most implicit faith and confidence. He was a highly valued member of the local Presbyterian Church and contributed liberally towards it.[2] The elder Stennis was a "gentleman farmer," depending on sharecroppers to tend the land. He judged the quality of his farmers on how straight they could guide their mule pulling a wooden-handled one-bottom plow. Young Stennis would later use his father's reasoning to judge his own actions.

In 1909 the family moved to DeKalb. Receiving a good education was stressed in the Stennis family. As the youngest child, he received instruction and guidance from his brothers, Sam, Thomas Laurence and Hampton Alexander, and his sisters, Annie, Bessie, and Janie. Mary Stennis, a first cousin, was the DeKalb school principal, and John's older sister, Bessie, was his teacher. Like many schools of the era, two or three grades were taught in the same room. Bessie was a good but strict teacher who believed in "study and preparation." Taking his sister's tenets to heart, young John had the reputation of being at the head of his class.

But John Stennis's life was not all school and lessons. While his leadership qualities were emerging, Stennis was enjoying his youth. He played baseball, swam in nearby creeks with Indian names like Sucarnooche or

Stennis as a small boy playing with a dog and a hog near his home in DeKalb, Mississippi.
(Courtesy Kemper County Historical Association)

Powticfaw, attended the Presbyterian Church, and enjoyed the companion-ship of his friends and neighbors. He once commented that although the family had few material possessions, their good friends and neighbors who shared a community spirit meant much more than money. John, however, was probably more privileged than most. His family was prominent in DeKalb. He was also more studious than some of his friends, who spent their spare time chewing tobacco and shooting dice. While they were out on the streets, John was at home studying or working in the drug store.[3]

DeKalb, located in east central Mississippi, was similar to most hill counties as roads ran along ridges and creek bottoms alternated with farms and forests. The scenery was certainly not so spectacular that tourists would visit. Yet, it was where young John Stennis had his roots. DeKalb is a small town with the two-story courthouse on the square surrounded by businesses. Streets would be full on Saturdays when the country folk came to town to shop. Having little money, many would come only to "see and be seen." With a festival atmosphere the stores would stay open late in the evening to serve the last customer. The Stennis name appeared above the doors of some of those businesses. John's family's house, a large white residence, was a block east of the square, so the town was not only his playground but a place where he could interact with its citizens. The pace of life was slow by today's standards.

At the age of 14, Stennis started working in the Stennis Rexall Drug Company operated by his brother, Hampton A. Stennis, nicknamed "Cap." The drug store was sandwiched between Hopper's Café and Little's Grocery. Young Stennis was the "soda jerk" manning the soda fountain that provided refreshments for those waiting for prescriptions to be filled. As the only ice cream parlor in town, the store was busy. According to a friend, John was fairly adept at flipping a glass in the air, catching it, mixing the cola drink, and sliding it down the bar to the waiting customer.[4] The fountain was also the gathering place for local businessmen taking a break from their offices and stores. Working behind the counter gave Stennis an opportunity to bet-ter know customers' views on local and national politics. He could have witnessed some heated debates there and in the courthouse as well.

The drug store was near the courthouse, and when court was in session Stennis would sit in the courthouse gallery to hear cases being tried. In addition, visiting attorneys from nearby Meridian would often visit the counter during recesses. Hearing attorneys discuss their cases and seeing them in action in the courtroom stimulated his interest in practicing law. Stennis learned more about a lawyer's life when he spent one summer with his older brother, Sam D. Stennis, who was an attorney in the Stennis and Osborne firm in Pampa, Texas. Not knowing exactly what he wanted to do, John considered studying medicine like his uncle, farming like his father, or becoming a pharmacist like his brother. However, his developing love for the law and his concern for other people swayed him. Certainly he made the right decision. Later he talked of his sixty years of public service, "I like people and I'm interested in them—that's the main reason I've stayed in public life all these years."[5]

Since the DaKalb School only went to the eleventh grade and was not accredited, Stennis attended eighth grade boarding school at the Kemper County Agricultural High School at nearby Scooba. That school, founded in 1913, became East Mississippi Junior College in 1927.

Sent Away

The decision to send young Stennis to another school surprised him. One night he came home from the drug store and found his mother darning a pair of his socks. He asked her why she was working on them at night. She told him that in the morning he would be catching the train to Scooba to start school there. He said he didn't want to move to another school, but she said, "Your father has spoken."[6] Stennis's father had wanted to be a doctor, but financial hardships resulting from the Civil War had made this impossible. He would make sure that John had the educational background necessary to attend college.

The distance from DeKalb to Scooba is only twelve miles, but travel at that time was difficult. The roads were dirt with no gravel and in the winter became almost impassable. The poor roads combined with slow travel by horse and buggy, or wagon, made this a day-long trip. When the railroad from DeKalb to Sucarnooche was built, connections could be made on the Mobile and Ohio railroad for travel north to Scooba.

Growing up as the youngest in the household, John was "considered juvenile and immature by his brothers. He developed a natural inclination towards an inquisitive and somewhat mischievous frame of mind, but always with a sense of fairness and consideration. His ethical standards were never compromised."[7] Living in the dormitory at Scooba, John had spare time to spend on something besides studying.

During the winter of 1918-1919 when nearly a foot of snow fell, classes were cancelled. Any snow was rare, but that amount not only slowed school activities, but it made the normally elusive rabbits easily gathered. A group of the students, including Stennis, caught about forty rabbits and put them in a dormitory room. When an instructor opened the door to the room, he was overrun by escaping rabbits.

In another prank, John fashioned a water gun from a piece of cane. He constructed a plunger by wrapping a string around a stick. With a small hole in the end, the long-range water gun was effective in cooling a budding romance. A visiting teacher from DeKalb was vying for the attention of the piano teacher. As it happened, John's agriculture teacher was also romantically interested in the piano teacher. To make the visiting teacher's stay as uncomfortable as possible, John and his roommate decided to test the water gun's effectiveness. After a few strategic squirts through his screen, the visitor closed his window even though it was hot and humid on that particular night.

For their involvement in that escapade, Stennis and his roommate had to dig and remove a pine stump on campus in full view of the girl's home economics class.

Like any typical teenager, he participated in such practical jokes, but he condemned any damaging actions of his peers.[8]

To break the monotony of the school's meals, John and his schoolmates would often forage the neighboring farms. They visited sugar cane and peanut fields, as well as pecan and fruit orchards, to ensure that nothing edible was wasted. They might also catch a chicken or collect eggs for a meal.[9]

Squirting visiting teachers with water and stealing eggs from the henhouse were juvenile activities Stennis participated in, but most of his time was structured and busy. Entertainment at school included occasional lectures, music recitals, athletic events, and a rare motion picture. Radio and television sets were non-existent. A passing airplane was so unusual that all of the boys would hurriedly lean out of the classroom window to get a glimpse.[10] John's primary sport was baseball, where he earned a few sore fingers, and was happily designated the team's catcher.

Stennis took courses in English, history, arithmetic, algebra, plane geometry, chemistry, agriculture, general science, Latin, physiology, and physical geography. He finished the required work but did not reach the academic level attained by one of the females at the school.[11] In his senior year, he was Class Prophet and president of the Hi-Y Club.[12] Along with his twenty classmates Stennis graduated with fifteen and one-half credits on May 12, 1919.

Mississippi A&M

He was now prepared to enter Mississippi A&M near Starkville. Although the college was only seventy miles away, he had to change trains three times to get there. His A&M experiences would set him on the path of public service.

Being away from home in high school had prepared Stennis for the structured college life at A&M. The day's activities, including meals, were all planned. Permits, which were given sparingly, were required to leave campus. Lights had to be out at ten each night.[13] Having an electric light to turn off and on and an indoor toilet were new experiences for most of the rural students like Stennis. Despite the rigid schedule, students felt privileged to be there. According to a friend who attended A&M, It was one place they didn't ask you how much money you had or what church you belonged to. Those who could dance would get out in the halls of Main Dormitory to teach the other boys the basic steps.[14]

Coming from farms, many of the young men attending A&M did not possess all of the social graces expected of a college student. But A&M embraced this kind of student. The college was established on February 28, 1878, as one of the land grant institutions under the Morrill Act of 1862. All land grant institutions promoted "scientific investigation and experimentation respecting the principles and applications of agricultural science" to those who would not otherwise have had access to universities.

Stennis entered Mississippi A&M on September 14, 1919, in the School of Agriculture. At this time he was preparing to become a farmer like his father. He took basic agricultural courses such as types and breeds of livestock, farm woodwork, poultry, farm mechanics, and agronomy. These classes were rounded out with the other required classes in literature, history, physical education, and military science.

Turner Catledge, who entered A&M one year before Stennis, became one of his close friends. Catledge chose A&M because the rooms were free, and jobs were available to pay for meals. Since A&M was a military school, uniforms were furnished, so Catledge knew he would not need a large wardrobe. According to him, Stennis, unlike most of the other students, had nice clothes which he willingly loaned to others when they left campus for dates and other outings. Stennis's mother had always insisted he dress appropriately, look nice, and do his best. Sharing clothes certainly did not diminish his popularity. Catledge knew early on that Stennis would succeed. He characterized him as "an outstanding student, a persuasive speaker, and a born politician even at age seventeen."[15]

Hazing of freshmen students was a popular sport for upperclassmen that even Stennis could not avoid. Freshmen were at the greatest risk when nothing else was going on and upperclassmen were bored. To hide from the juniors and seniors one particularly boring Saturday afternoon, John and his roommate gained entrance to the Agricultural Engineering building and decided to take a nap on the drafting tables, only to be startled when someone started a piece of farm machinery.[16] In another hazing incident, a friend stood on the ledge outside the window of his third-story room in Main Dormitory to escape the upperclassmen.[17] Apparently the administration did not consider roughing up freshmen a serious offense.

All A&M students participated in the military science program. Stennis, not surprisingly, took the military science program seriously. By graduation, he was a cadet captain leading Company D. He spent six weeks in the summer of 1922 at Camp McClellan, Alabama, training with students from the University of Alabama, the Citadel, Louisiana State University, Oglethorpe, University of Florida, and Clemson. Military tactics and physical conditioning were a part of the training. During the training Stennis was "A&M's unofficial ambassador for intercollegiate relationships."[18] In his second year he was a corporal and in his junior year he was promoted to first sergeant in the military science program and president of the First Sergeant's Club. During his first three terms at A&M he also took science courses in botany, taxonomy, morphology, and physics. Surprisingly, he earned higher grades in the science courses than in the agricultural courses. With encouragement from chemistry professors Herbert Johnson Smith and Williams Flowers Hand, he transferred to the School of Science in 1920.

Stennis did very well in his science courses, earning grades mostly in the 80s with a few 70s and 90s. He was awarded his highest grade, a 94, in elementary physics and his lowest, a 69, in general geology. For a foreign language, he chose German.

As a science major, he took seven chemistry courses, and in one of those chemistry classes he demonstrated his leadership abilities. One student in the analytical chemistry class always sat in the seat nearest the door so he could make a quick exit after class. The other students felt that they should take turns sitting in that particular seat.

One day before class a small scuffle ensued and in the pushing incident, the professor's laboratory demonstration was damaged. When Professor

Smith entered the laboratory, Stennis accepted blame for the incident and promised to repair the damage. Taking the blame for his fellow students undoubtedly solidified friendships, but also indicated his abilities to calm a potentially confrontational situation between the students and teacher.[19] Many times in his career, he would step forward when the future of the country rather than a few broken test tubes was at stake.

At A&M, students held a "kangaroo court" to administer disciplinary actions for activities they believed damaged the college. They brought accused students before their court, and punishments could be severe. In one of the court sessions, Stennis learned a valuable lesson. After the court had charged a student with disrespect for authority they passed judgment and sentenced him. Shortly thereafter an older student, Bob Morrow, entered the room. Morrow, a World War I veteran, was considered by the younger students to be a "man among boys."[20] This was a fitting title since he was one of the few young commissioned officers in that conflict. When he reviewed the case with them, he advised that much of the evidence presented was "hearsay" and could not be used. Seeing both sides of this incident made an impression on Stennis, and he now knew that he wanted to become a lawyer.

In a few short years, he would look to Bob Morrow for more advice when he chose Morrow as his campaign manager in his pivotal race for public office.

It was by sheer chance Stennis's life was influenced by another A&M faculty member. While sitting on the steps of Lee Hall one day, through the open windows behind him Stennis heard one of Professor Alfred Benjamin Butts's lectures on political science. Butts's presentation reinforced his desire for public service. As a result, he enrolled in Butts's American government course, earning a grade of 86.

Stennis was always involved in campus activities and when he did not make the football team, he did the next best thing by becoming a cheerleader. In his senior year, he was elected head cheerleader. He again demonstrated evolving leadership traits when the team played the University of

Tennessee at Memphis in 1922. Stennis ushered the band off the bus and, along with the other cheerleaders, led them down Main Street in an impromptu parade to celebrate the game.[21] He did not have a parade permit, but no one seemed to notice. The "M Club" thanked him for rallying the students behind the Bulldogs by soliciting funds to buy him a white sweater with an embossed megaphone.

John Stennis also led the cheerleaders in welcoming the female students from nearby Mississippi State College for Women in Columbus during their annual visit to A&M. They arrived by rail in a ten-car train dubbed the "Magnolia Special." As they left the train for Lee Hall, the young ladies formed two lines and walked toward the center of the drill field in the middle of the campus. The Maroon Band played, and the "W" students sang their alma mater. John and the other cheerleaders replied with a few cheers and songs which were "more lustily but much less musically given."

The 1923 A&M yearbook, *Reveille*, described Stennis's cheerleading thusly:

> No history making events have featured the Aggie Athletic calendar this year, but the student body supported its teams better than ever before. Through the fabric of this splendid spirit that has sprung into being runs the crimson thread of courage and pep that is John [Stennis]. A leader in every activity that attracted his attention. He practically put the Memphis trip across single-handed and helped to give us the best *Reflector* that ever saw a printer's ink. But read his record, it speaks for itself.[22]

Throughout his collegiate career, Stennis was known to be a hard worker, very popular, and "far above the average student."[23] In addition to being head cheerleader and the Business Manager for the *Reflector*, he was Life Secretary for the Senior Class of 1923, Secretary of the Gordians, a senior honorary society, and president of the Kemper County Club.

At the 1923 Gordians's banquet, Bob Morrow presented the program, "Possibilities of the Gordians." Morrow's program was prophetic: classmate and Toastmaster Turner Catledge, who later became Managing Editor for the *New York Times*; Ben Hilbun, whom Stennis narrowly defeated for "Most Popular," who served as Mississippi State University's eleventh president; and Stennis, who became Mississippi's statesman in the U. S. Senate.

Stennis was also a member of the First Sergeants Club and the Salmagundi Club. The 1923 yearbook recognized his outgoing personality with the following: "He is an ardent believer in the philosophy of the smiling face, and John's beaming countenance and cherry 'Hello' have served to lift many a student from the throes of that proverbial malady called the 'blues.'"[24] Stennis also received recognition for his hard work, but he preferred following the class motto: "Build for Character, Not for Fame." Coincidently, his high school class motto and school colors of maroon and white were the same as those of A&M. But he had changed. The mischievous nature he had in high school was gone. He assumed a serious countenance anticipating the responsibilities he would tackle in the future. He graduated from A&M on June 4, 1923.

Law School

In 1924 Stennis entered the University of Virginia Law School at Charlottesville, Virginia. He was accepted after an interview with the dean without ever completing an application. Here he could study in the shadows of two of the school's founding fathers whom he respected and admired, James Madison and Thomas Jefferson, whose home at Monticello he visited many times. He read their biographies as well as the biographies of other famous leaders like Benjamin Franklin, Robert E. Lee, and George Washington, and patterned his future life of public service after them.

Law school was difficult the first year, "I felt that I wasn't as prepared as some of the students. I had to work very hard to keep up, but I was determined to succeed." On one occasion he remained at school during Christmas holidays to study intensively the U.S. Constitution. He surprised himself and his classmates one day. While citing a constitutional question, he recited the entire document![25] He was enamored with the American system of government and would spend the rest of his life supporting and defending it. His hard work paid off as he earned a Phi Beta Kappa key for his scholastic achievements.

Due to illness at home, Stennis took a leave of absence from law school. While he was at home, an incumbent in the Mississippi legislature passed away, creating a vacancy in the House. Dr. Bell, a local doctor, advised Stennis to run for the office. Upon contemplating this idea, Stennis replied that he would face some obstacles in this race. To which the doctor replied, "Young man, there are always going to be some obstacles."[26]

Mississippi Legislature

Following the doctor's advice he was elected to the Mississippi House of Representatives, taking office in January 1928.

He would soon meet two others in Mississippi government who would impact his career: Theodore G. Bilbo, the current governor, and James O. Eastland, also a member of the legislature.

As governor, Bilbo planned to call the legislature into session in 1931 to consider several initiatives, some of which Stennis opposed. Stennis, unlike Bilbo, was not one to speak unkindly about anyone and had little in common with the governor. When Bilbo came to DeKalb for a political rally, Stennis reluctantly let his son, John Hampton, listen from the Bell Hotel balcony.[27] When Bilbo requested legislation against Stennis's principles, he replied:

> I entered the Legislature high of hope, tolerant, patient, eagerly seeking a chance for humble service. Mine is and has been the idea that my commission was not a thing personal to me, but was merely a delegation of power from the people, held in trust, to be exercised for their benefit. The experiences encountered during my feeble efforts in the last four sessions has been quite disillusioning. However, with a great deal of humble satisfaction in my heart I can sincerely say that I have measured every single question on its own merit as presented, with no ulterior motive, then or thereafter. This is the simple rule of conduct, as I understand it, pre-

scribed by the people who gave me the trust and was assumed by me in my oath. As this simple ideal has been my guide heretofore, it is the sole idea in mind as I humbly approach the grave task of passing matters recently presented…When I took my oath of office, I meant it.[28]

During his four years in the Mississippi House, Stennis served on the Immigration and Labor Committee; Public Printing Committee; Railroads Committee; Roads, Ferries, and Bridges Committee; Judiciary En Banc Committee; Division B; and Joint Committee on Enrolled Bills. During his tenure he proposed bills dealing with pensions, education, public utilities, and group insurance.[29] Stennis always supported projects that would improve the quality of life among his fellow Mississippians. He often said that making a living was the greatest problem faced by most Mississippians. Many things, now taken for granted, such as paved roads and electricity did not exist in rural Mississippi during the Stennis era in the Mississippi House. Later, as a U. S. Senator, he would have the opportunity to help move the state into the twentieth century.

In 1928, after attending to the family business, Stennis returned to the University of Virginia to complete his law degree. He once commented that he came back to Mississippi from the University of Virginia with a law degree on one train and the Depression arrived on the next.[30]

Back Home

On December 24, 1929, Stennis married Coy Hines from Union County, Mississippi. She was employed as the Kemper County Home Economist, after attending State Teachers College, which later became the University of Southern Mississippi. While still a student there, she met Stennis on a visit to A&M. She too had come from a large family—thirteen children—all of whom grew up in the Pleasant Ridge community near Dumas, Mississippi, and Coy was the only offspring in her family to attend college. Her father, John Wesley Hines, farmed and operated a country store. After they married, Stennis and "Miss Coy," as she came to be known, built a wood frame house in DeKalb on Highway 39. The house still stands today and is home to Stennis's daughter, Margaret.

During the Depression, cotton prices were down to four and one-half cents a pound. Other commodities were low as well. Banks closed. A few businesses failed. However, the resilient Kemper County residents grew their own food and helped each other through the hard times. According to some, they did not have much to lose and did not need much to survive. Without money Kemper folk could not pay attorney fees, and Stennis was forced to seek a position with a steady income.

District Attorney John C. Stennis

In 1931, when the district attorney's office for the sixteenth judicial district became available, Stennis ran against B. Frank Bell and won with over a two-to-one vote margin.

As with anything he did, he gave the office his best efforts. Passersby could see him in his office at night, there in the second-story window of the courthouse, practicing his arguments for an upcoming case before a mirror. According to his friend, J. C. Warren, "He prepared his cases, doggone man, he prepared them. When he got up, he addressed that courtroom; he knew what he was talking about. He really prepared them."[31]

One case prosecuted by Stennis in March 1934 reached the U. S. Supreme Court. Three black men—Henry Shields, Yank Ellington, and Ed Brown—were tried for the murder of a white planter named Raymond Stewart. To prevent mob violence and a possible lynching, the trio was quickly brought to trial after confessions were obtained by violent, unscrupulous means. The men were beaten, threatened with hanging and whipped so severely that one defendant had to stand as he was too sore to sit. After having the coerced confessions entered as evidence, District Attorney John Stennis successfully prosecuted the case and obtained a guilty verdict of capital murder. The three were scheduled to be hanged in DeKalb May 11,

Stennis successfully ran for Mississippi's Sixteenth Judicial District Attorney's office in 1931. In his sixty years of public service he never lost an election. (Courtesy Kemper County Historical Association)

1934. While the gallows were being constructed, one of the court-appointed defense lawyers, John A. Clark, filed for an appeal to the Mississippi Supreme Court. When the state upheld the lower court's findings, the case was appealed by former Mississippi Governor Earl Brewer to the U. S. Supreme Court. Citing coerced confessions, the lower court's decisions were reversed. Faced with the cost of a new trial and the lack of physical evidence, Stennis and Brewer compromised on manslaughter charges. The defendants were given credit for time served while their case was being challenged.[32]

At the time of the trial, Clark was serving in the Mississippi Senate, but he was defeated in the next election in 1935 because of his support of the blacks. In addition to ending his political career, the trial and its aftermath caused him to have a mental breakdown.[33] The editor of the *Kemper County Messenger* "congratulated" Stennis after the trial, writing that a "good legal hanging would be the greatest crime deterrent possible."[34] Stennis had wanted to retry the case, but after confessions had been obtained, the evidence was not preserved. When the expense of a new trial was considered, the compromise appeared reasonable.

While Stennis knew the defendants had been beaten, he defended his prosecutorial position by stating that no court officials were involved. However, court records did show that deputy sheriffs participated in the beatings. Rather than retry the defendants, they were allowed to plead to manslaughter charges. The defendants chose the shorter terms in prison, fearing that in a retrial they could again face the death penalty. Whether Stennis believed the trio guilty, or that any leniency toward the blacks would terminate his political career as it had Clark's is not known. By siding with those who beat the defendants, Stennis, unlike Clark, appears to have abandoned his principles of justice. Regardless, the Democratic executive committee certainly believed that he had fulfilled his duties; they nominated him as their district attorney candidate in 1935, declaring that, "John Stennis meets the high Jeffersonian standards for public service: 'He is honest, he is diligent, he is capable. No finer tribute could be paid to any public official.'"[35]

On March 2, 1935, John Hampton Stennis was born. Called "Hamp" by his father, he would later accompany his dad, who was canvassing the state in his bid for a senate seat. Following in his father's footsteps, he attended the University of Virginia to earn a law degree. Deciding to enter politics, he was elected to the Mississippi House of Representatives, serving from 1964 to 1984. Choosing to practice law in Mississippi as a partner in the firm of Watkins, Ludlam, Winter, and Stennis, he remained a valuable political consultant to his father.

On November 20, 1937, a daughter, Margaret Jane, was born. Stennis nicknamed her "MJ." She remembers many frontyard softball games for young children in the neighborhood with Dad serving as pitcher. He also taught her to swim in nearby Sucarnooche Creek, telling her to "kick and knock." Rather than politics, Margaret chose a future in education, earning a degree from Duke University. She spent most of her adult years in North and South Carolina, but moved back to Mississippi in 1996 to live in the house John and Coy had built in DeKalb.

Judge Stennis

In 1937, when the Circuit Judge for John Stennis's district, W. W. MaGruder of Starkville, died, Stennis was appointed by Governor Hugh White to fill the vacancy. At that time he was one of the youngest men to wear the robes of a Mississippi judge.[36] Later, he successfully ran for the judgeship and was twice re-elected without opposition. When the time neared for the judge's election he sent a note to the members of the bar in the sixteenth judicial district asking for their support. At the same time, he told them that whether they supported him or not it would have no bearing on future cases should he be elected:

> Within the next few weeks there will be a campaign in your district for Circuit Judge. If you see fit to support anyone, I shall be very glad to have that effort. However, I shall not embarrass you in any way by seeking an expression from you. I do not think a lawyer should be called on to

take any part in the campaign, but if he sees fit to take a part, this is certainly his privilege. If you do take a part, be that in my favor or not in my favor, there will be no hereafter about it with me. If you do not take part, there will be no hereafter about it with me. I have enjoyed serving as a fellow officer with you in your Circuit Court. If I deserve to be elected, I will be, if I do not, I will not be. But if I am reelected, it will be without any official obligation to any person, or group of persons.[37]

In a case involving Choctaw Chief Cameron Wesley, who was charged with killing another Choctaw, the Circuit Court acquitted the Chief. Wesley was then tried in Choctaw court, where the penalty was death. The Choctaw court also acquitted him, thereby substantiating the jury's judgment. Stennis, who was very interested in any venue of the law, visited the Choctaw court during that trial.[38] He was pleased that their decision matched his. He won the respect of the Choctaws and would later support legislation benefiting them while in the Senate.

As a judge Stennis conducted an orderly court. During his tenure as judge, Stennis never had a civil case overturned. Attorney J. P. Coleman, who would later become a good friend and advisor, first saw John Stennis when he filed a claim in circuit court in Oktibbeha County. After the session he noted, "This is a most unusual man, highly polished, he know[s] his business, very dignified, ran an orderly court, one that I have been waiting to see for a very long time…He just impressed everybody from A to Z."[39] According to J. C. Warren, a friend, Stennis had "decorum, my gosh, he didn't have anything but law and order in the courtroom, you know, he demanded it and he got it."[40]

He expected all members of the court to respect the judicial system. Once, when a highway patrolman was late for 9:00 AM court because he was across the street drinking coffee, Stennis asked him, "Did you think I was going to conduct court in the café across the street?"

The officer answered, "No sir."

Stennis then told him, "Tomorrow you be in your place at sixty minutes after eight o'clock."[41]

Stennis presented the duties of court officers in a small pamphlet he wrote for prospective jurors:

> A great Democrat, Grover Cleveland, once said, "A public office is a public trust." No one has ever spoken a greater truth in so few words; and no one has ever given a better, nor a more lofty definition of a public office.
>
> I have frequently observed that people will not have much respect for the laws if that law is represented by individuals they do not respect. All of us who are officers have peculiar responsibilities. The eyes of the people, particularly the eyes of the youth of the country, are directly on us. We were not compelled to take the offices we hold. We assumed the obligations and we receive the pay. Let all of us strive, day in and day out, to do our duty, fairly and honorably, regardless of consequences to self or to others. Let us strive daily to be a worthy part of the machinery of justice in your county. An officer cannot always please the people, but he can always have what is far more valuable, their respect and his self respect.[42]

Stennis always had the highest regard for judges and considered it one of his highest honors to represent the people of his district as circuit judge. He formed lasting friendships with those in the county courthouses and never failed to stop to visit when he passed through.[43]

A leisurely Sunday afternoon automobile ride often highlighted the week for some of DeKalb's residents. Daughter Margaret recalled that on one of those drives, the Stennis family was flagged down by a man sitting on a downtown bench, "Mr. John, Mr. John, the Japs have bombed us!" The date was December 7, 1941. They rushed home to hear more about the attack on Pearl Harbor on the radio.

Now at war, Stennis hoped to use his college military training in support of the war effort. He wrote the Navy Department in New Orleans, and they sent him to Birmingham for a physical exam. According to a letter he wrote to a friend, Hubert Scrivener, who had worked with him in the drug store, doctors found a small hernia [ulcer.] [They] "turned me down, much to my disappointment, and now I feel useless, but I wish I could do something in some small way."[44]

Determined to join the fight, he went back to Birmingham, where Dr. Seale Harris told him to give up cigarettes and begin a diet of milk and orange juice so that the ulcer could heal. He wrote his attorney friend John McCully, who was in the service, that giving up both smoking and eating was quite a challenge, stating that the next time he had to sentence a man to prison he would just give him his freedom but forbid him to smoke. Dr. Seale advised this treatment would take sixty to ninety days and would require Stennis to remain in bed part of the day.

During this time he decided to run for a higher office than circuit judge.[45] Still under doctor's orders, Stennis missed an opportunity to run for Congress when U. S. Senator Pat Harrison died on June 22, 1941. James O. Eastland was appointed by Governor Paul Johnson to complete Harrison's term, but did not run in the special election held in September 1941. Wall Doxey from Holly Springs defeated Ross A. Collins in that special election. Eastland successfully ran the following August 1942, leading both Doxey and Collins in the first primary and defeating Doxey in the second primary.[46] Stennis felt that anyone educated by the government should serve in the military, and he was annoyed that Eastland, who had not served, was elected.[47]

At the time, he still believed he might be able to join one of the armed forces. After failing another physical, however, he knew he could not serve in the military. Stennis was frustrated when he could not get into the service in World War II. He wanted to serve on the front lines where the action was and made several attempts at joining but an ulcer prevented enlistment. He knew that he somehow could use the training he received in the ROTC program at Mississippi A&M.

On the Home Front

Undeterred, he revived his cheerleader experiences in order to boost the spirits of servicemen from Kemper County by printing a monthly newsletter entitled "On the Beam." The first issue was mailed November 5, 1943. This paper presented the "news of chaff and chatter that ordinarily does not find its way to newspapers nor otherwise get the recognition or dignity of being written up." He wrote about the weather and the crops and described what was happening as he made a tour about town.

A typical article for "On the Beam" read like this: "Let's take a swing around town and see what we shall see, beginning with Barber Knight, who I see whacking away, without enough fire in his stove, sitting on his old about-to-fall-down stool while he gives someone a first class haircut that is hard to beat. Incidentally, he is 'America's only sitting down barber' and mail so addressed will reach him."[48]

Along with the local news he expressed the community's thankfulness for the servicemen's sacrifices. He implored them to seek a total victory so that their sons would not have to go to war later on. Many soldiers responded to the newsletter stating that receiving one was the next best thing to a trip home. Stennis's newsletter encouraged and inspired the troops and at the same time gave them both good and bad news, along with some homespun humor. While he extolled their service, he expected them to make their own opportunities upon their return.

> To those of you who are really fighting this war, you can never be repaid. However, do not place your hope for happiness in the future on government aid by whatever name called. The government can give you an opportunity (and it will and should do this); but it cannot bring you happiness. Only you can do that. It cannot bring you the worthwhile satisfactions of life. Even your parents cannot do that. Only you, by your own efforts, and by your own achievements, can bring the real happiness and the real satisfactions. Do not cheat yourself by letting anyone lead you to believe otherwise.[49]

Stennis believed that an individual's success and happiness were self-determined. For that reason, he would later oppose many of the Great Society programs of the 1960s. As the end of World War II was in sight, he maintained that only a strong military would prevent future wars. At that time he did not realize that in the future he would have the power to ensure that strength:

> We must have the army, the navy, and the air force and all that goes with all departments, all so big and strong that no nation or combination of nations will dare attack us. We must remember that in our day and for many generations to come, disarmament is not the road to peace; it is an open invitation to war. The productive power and the fighting men of the U.S. saved the world this time; the next time if we are not prepared, they will attack us first and there will be no time to get ready. We must stay ready and we shall.[50]

Seeking a Higher Office

As the war plodded on, Stennis's reputation as a fair judge began to spread. Soon his supporters begged him to run for higher office, possibly the governorship or lieutenant governorship. He carefully considered running for governor but was not interested in the lieutenant governor's office. In a late winter's night session with neighboring Judge J. P. Coleman in 1945, it was agreed that Coleman would be better suited to the governorship with all of the politics involved; while the intellectual scholar, Stennis, could better serve in the U. S. Senate.

At this time, several monumental problems were developing with the current U. S. Senator, Theodore G. Bilbo. Bilbo's health was declining and his fellow senators had barred him from taking his seat. These two major events encouraged Stennis to consider running for the Senate.

Bilbo was an embarrassment to the other senators. His venomous remarks on the race issue played well to some in Mississippi, but not to his fellow senators and certainly not to all Mississippians. For his actions, the Senate refused to seat him at the beginning of the 80th Congressional Session in 1947. He was charged with disfranchisement of black voters by intimidation, and some serious accusations were made about his use of defense contractors on his farm near Poplarville, Mississippi. Bilbo, who referred to himself as "The Man," enjoyed a controversial situation; he was eager to fight for his seat. He had received a 1946 Cadillac from one defense contractor as a Christmas gift and when questioned, replied that "it was just an old Southern custom."[51] At one hearing a black resident testified that Bilbo's speeches made him afraid to vote.

In January 1947, Stennis visited Mississippi Governor Fielding Wright to gauge the Governor's reaction to Bilbo's problems and to discover how he planned to fill the vacancy should Bilbo be refused a seat. Wright told Stennis that if Bilbo was found guilty on the illegal use of government contractors he would appoint a replacement, but if he were charged with disfranchisement, he would re-appoint him. In the next senatorial election, Wright told Stennis he would be a good candidate "with the best chance to win" since the "people would look for a clean, middle aged man whom they thought could restore prestige to the state."[52]

After his visit with Wright, a story in the Jackson, Mississippi paper, *The Clarion Ledger*, on April 11, 1947, mentioned that Stennis was Wright's choice for the appointment to Bilbo's seat in the Senate. Stennis, disturbed by the story, quickly wrote Wright and Bilbo denying any responsibility for it. Wright responded to Stennis's letter, stating that he knew Stennis would not talk to the press about their conversation.

Bilbo had personal problems that overshadowed his fight with the U. S. Senate. He told Stennis that he was not concerned about the *Clarion Ledger* article; he was having health problems.[53] Bilbo, a small man just over five feet tall, often wore a red tie held in place by a horseshoe-shaped, diamond stickpin to symbolize the "rednecks" he represented. He was seldom seen without a cigar in his mouth. From this smoking habit, he developed cancer of the mouth and throat and died August 21, 1947. Bilbo's death created the vacancy that could give John C. Stennis his chance to seek a higher office by running for the U. S. Senate. It all depended on the actions of Governor Wright.

CHAPTER II
THE RACE FOR THE SENATE

When Mississippi Senator Pat Harrison died in 1941, John Stennis received many letters encouraging him to run for the vacancy. One letter stated, "You are young, capable, energetic, and have no political line ups… You have political friends but no political machine. It is my belief that you could have a good chance to be elected by carrying on just the type of campaign that elected you District Attorney. Whatever you may do, whether this or something else, I am with you."[1]

Another letter encouraged Stennis to seek the Senate seat, "I do not believe that this country has faced so critical a period in its history as it is now facing, and we need men of strong intellect and unimpeachable character to represent us in that august body, the United States Senate, and I know you measure up to that standard or I would not urge you to make the race."[2]

Stennis had planned to seek a higher political office and was rumored to be a probable gubernatorial candidate. Mississippi State alumni, anxious to gain state-wide recognition for the 1951 gubernatorial race, invited him to make speeches at various civic clubs and events. At many of these talks Stennis outlined his position supporting the formation of the United Nations.[3] In a letter to a supporter who had asked him to consider the lieutenant governorship, Stennis replied that he would not be interested in that position, "I have definitely decided, though, that sometime in the future I am going to run for some high office, stake everything on one effort; if elected, I shall continue in public service; but if defeated, I shall retire from public life to a private law practice."[4]

He had missed an opportunity to run for Congress by trying to get in the army. Bilbo's passing provided Stennis another opportunity. In a memo to his son, Stennis later stated, "For a number of years I had aspired to a seat in the United States Senate and knew the best time to run was when there was a vacancy."[5]

Stennis was holding court in Macon when he received the news that Senator Bilbo had died Thursday, August 21, 1947. Stennis did not attend Bilbo's funeral at Poplarville that following Saturday. Governor Wright, once rumored as a self-appointee to the Senate seat, announced immediately that there would be no appointments since the legislature was not in session. Former governor Hugh White wanted Wright to appoint him to finish the remaining five years of Bilbo's term, but Wright refused. Had Wright appointed White, it is doubtful that Stennis would have opposed him because White had appointed Stennis to the bench in 1937.[6]

Instead of an appointment, a plurality election would be held on November 4, 1947 to elect Mississippi's next U. S. Senator. There would be no run-off or second primary. It would be "winner takes all."

Following this election the law was changed to require runoffs, if needed, between the top two candidates.

Before entering the race, Stennis needed his wife's consent. She reluctantly agreed. Once he announced, she gave him her full support. His wife's connections with the Mississippi Cooperative Extension Service surely helped garner support from the agricultural community.

Concerned about health problems, Stennis also consulted his doctor, Dr. J.L. Hasie, who said he could "put me through" the election.[7]

Not wanting to be seen as coveting Bilbo's Senate seat, Stennis waited until after the funeral to announce his candidacy. Considered an unknown by most political observers, his election team announced the intentions of their candidate. His was the first name to go public Monday, August 25, 1947.

J.P. Coleman, who had earlier encouraged Stennis to seek a seat in the Senate, received a call on Sunday night, August 24. Stennis told him of his plan to announce the next day. Coleman later said, "Well, it gave me a real chill of some kind up and down my spine—not that I objected to his running, that is just exactly what I urged him to do. But I knew then and there that the battle was on and the time had come to deliver or else."[8]

Stennis's supporters knew that winning would be difficult, but they had unwavering faith in their candidate. Selected to be the campaign's publicity chairman, Erle Johnston, editor of the *Scott County Times*, was optimistic. "[Stennis] was the first to announce for the Bilbo vacancy. He will be the first to open his speaking campaign. He will also be the first when the returns come in on November 4. Not as widely known as some of the other candidates, Judge Stennis may have some disadvantages, but we are confident his name will be a household byword before the campaign is over. Wherever he speaks, he makes friends. He has a quality about him that inspires admiration and respect."[9]

In a campaign organizational meeting on September 5, seventeen men met at the Stennis campaign headquarters in the Edwards Hotel in Jackson to map an election strategy. As the group convened, the talk centered on Stennis's qualifications and character. Anxious to get to the crux of the meeting, his longtime friend, J.P. Coleman, abruptly halted the discussion by remarking, "We do not need to waste our time talking about the candidate. We already have him. What we need is money for this campaign." Then, the tall, outspoken Coleman strode to the front of the room and placed a $1000 check on the table. Following his lead, the remainder of the group, including S.R. Evans, Bob Morrow, Sam Wilhite, Harry McArthur, Buck Palmer, and J.E. Hall, contributed a like amount to kick off the campaign. Some years later, Stennis recalled:

> I ran for the U. S. Senate in 1947 more on a hope with a little prayer for light and guidance and virtually no money. That is where your friends come in. I had some fine hard-working, loyal, unselfish friends throughout the state. To use an old-fashioned political term, they really got out and beat the bushes. Their zeal and enthusiasm and determination, too, and their spirit of working for a cause and enlisting others in the work were what added up, a few votes here and a few votes there, until those few votes became many votes, and it finally added up to enough to win.[10]

From the beginning of the campaign Stennis knew he had an uphill battle, but he was undaunted.

> I thought that I had a fighting chance to be elected; and according to my philosophy, a fighting chance is all a person deserves in life because if people are not willing to fight and put themselves into their endeavors to the limit, they are not only going to escape much of a reward for themselves; but they will not make much of a contribution either.[11]

While Stennis was the first to announce, others soon entered the race. Two incumbent members of the U. S. House, William Colmer from Pascagoula and John Rankin from Tupelo, decided to run. Forest Jackson, who defended Bilbo's Senate charges of bribery and disenfranchisement, and Paul Johnson Jr., the son of the former governor also vied for the coveted seat. The lone Republican candidate was L.R. Collins.

Colmer, elected to the U. S. House of Representatives in 1932, was probably the best known and was favored by many to win. However, Paul Johnson Jr. was also from the Gulf Coast. His entrance into the race was certainly welcomed by the Stennis camp as it effectively split the coastal electorate.

A few years after the election, Paul Jr. commented on his dividing the South Mississippi vote by saying, "We elected a good Senator in 1947, didn't we?"[12]

During the campaign, the race issue was not prominently discussed. However, Forest Jackson held to Bilbo's racial philosophy as did Rankin, who claimed he would "out Bilbo Bilbo." Stennis presented no position on the race issue.[13]

Stennis's platform supported "agriculture, education, conservation of natural resources, and international affairs."[14] Stennis was a segregationist, but he had the support of black newspaper editor Percy Greene, who considered him a fair person. However, Greene was discouraged from publicly endorsing Stennis in his newspaper, the *Jackson Advocate*. The campaign staff believed Greene's endorsement might give opponents an opportunity to make race a major issue in the election.[15]

Stennis's campaign manager, Bob Morrow, had never managed a political campaign, but as a colonel in the U. S. Army in World War I, he was familiar with military campaigns. Being adjutant emeritus of the Mississippi American Legion, Morrow was well known to all veterans, and as an A&M graduate he was recognized by many Mississippi State alumni. Sticking with his military experiences, he devised a battle plan for the campaign. Morrow agreed to run the campaign only if: (1) Stennis would make no promises to anyone, (2) All advertisements and schedule of public speeches would be under his control, and (3) No big money would be accepted without his approval.

According to S.R. Evans, no big money was ever accepted. At the end of the election they were four thousand dollars in debt.[16] Several large donors offered to contribute after the votes were counted, but Morrow said they would collect from the original alliance, "We're not going to sell out to somebody that didn't support us."[17]

In return for his efforts, Morrow would accept neither pay nor a promise of any public office.[18] He said, "I would not manage anyone's campaign for money." Later, Stennis recollected that Morrow paid someone to run his auto dealership during the three month campaign and would not even let Stennis buy his breakfast.[19]

Other supporters put their personal goals aside to help Stennis. J.C. Warren quit his job as the Kemper County Chancery Court clerk in order to help. Another friend, Dr. Red Hughes, who played on A&M's basketball team when Stennis was a student, closed his orthodontic office in Jackson to help with the campaign effort. Hughes went "door to door" asking residents to vote for Stennis. The day after the election, he reopened his practice in the Lamar Life Building. Hughes wanted nothing for his services, nor did he want anything after the election.[20]

Supporters' love and devotion to Stennis played a huge part in his election. A Stennis supporter later commented:

I don't believe there's ever been a candidate in Mississippi that ever had as many people working for free as John Stennis had. Well, I always said that we had a good product. Now I don't mean this disparagingly against other folks, but we had the best candidate largely. We went in it for one thing. The only thing we were interested in was good government.[21]

Morrow selected Stennis's cousin, Jesse Stennis, and Sam Wilhite to head county efforts. W.S. "Pete" Mitchell was chosen to manage the Jackson office along with their office worker Lorraine Lowry. Erle Johnson started the campaign as publicity director but Frank Smith later assumed the post full time.[22]

There being no candidate from the Delta, Morrow focused his initial efforts there. In each of the counties, Morrow chose a "field man" to start a Stennis Club to solicit local support. Somewhat clandestinely formed, the Stennis Clubs were able to judge local politics and initiate crucial contacts well before other candidates organized.[23]

Morrow developed a unique system of polling the state to judge campaign effectiveness. Campaign workers traveled to a Delta town and discussed politics with people they met in cafes, service stations, and other public places. Instead of asking for Stennis's support, the workers asked those they met about their voting intentions. Later, as the campaign progressed, other workers would visit the same town to see if the voters' intentions had changed. When campaign workers placed ads in local papers, they would also discuss the upcoming election in an attempt to gauge local voters' preferences.

To create the perception that Stennis's support was widespread, several cars displaying Stennis posters on their doors would drive through the Delta towns. When one potential voter was polled, he stated that with so many people for Stennis, he must be the one everyone was supporting. Clearly Morrow's strategies were effective. The Stennis name was being mentioned more frequently.[24]

Morrow seized every chance to promote his candidate. He recognized a unique opportunity in a Memphis *Commercial Appeal* article. A story was published with a strategy analogous to a tactic used by Mississippi Representative John Allen in the 1885 election for the U. S. House of Representatives. A former officer in the Confederacy, General William F. Tucker, told the voters they should not vote for Allen, who was only a private. Allen countered by asking all of the voters who were generals to vote for his opponent, while the privates who were guarding the generals should vote for him. Allen won the election and gained the title, "Private" John Allen.

Mississippi legislative leaders from the Delta including Mississippi's powerful speaker of the house, Walter Sillers, a Colmer supporter, left the state during the 1947 campaign for a goose hunt in Canada. A picture of them boarding the plane in Memphis accompanied by a story on their support for Colmer appeared in the *Commercial Appeal*. The Stennis team took advantage of the situation by saying, "All of the voters who could afford to go to Canada to hunt should vote for Colmer, while those Mississippians who couldn't afford a Canadian hunting trip, who had to stay home hunting rabbits and squirrels, should vote for Stennis."[25]

Newspaper endorsements gave candidates an edge in winning the election. In the beginning most newspapers requested candidates to conduct a fair campaign without racial overtones.

As time went on, newspapers began backing specific candidates. In general, they were universal in one theme—the state did not need another Bilbo. At the same time, an anti-Bilbo stance was not sufficient for winning an election. Stennis was endorsed immediately by DeKalb's *Kemper County Messenger*, followed by Greenwood's *Morning Star*, Tunica's *Times-Democrat*, Greenville's *Delta Democrat Times*, Houston's *Times-Post*, Oxford's *Eagle*, Louisville's *Winston County Journal*, New Albany's *Gazette*, Eupora's *Webster Progress*, Mark's *Quitman County Democrat*, Forest's *Scott County Times*, Cleveland's *Bolivar Commercial*, Grenada's *Grenada County Weekly*, Vicksburg's *Evening Post*, Newton's *Record*, Prentiss's *Highlight*, Starkville's *News*, and Macon's *Beacon*. The Columbus *Commercial Dispatch* and the West Point *Daily Times Leader* did not endorse anyone, while the Aberdeen *Examiner* chose to support Rankin. Stennis commented that some newspapers said, "He was a worker, but rather dull."

Colmer received support from the *Jackson Daily News*, Rosedale's *Bolivar Democrat*, and the *Commercial Appeal*, but another newspaper in his district, the *Gulfport-Biloxi Herald* remained uncommitted. The *Clarion Ledger*, the newspaper with the largest circulation, supported Paul Johnson while his hometown Hattiesburg paper, *American*, was uncommitted.

While Stennis's supporters lacked political campaign experience, their candidate was becoming widely recognized by the voters.

By this time, Mississippi A&M adopted a new name, Mississippi State College. The A&M alumni were still loyal and played an important part in the Stennis campaign. Stennis had been active in alumni affairs, even serving as alumni president. In addition to A&M alumni, Stennis supporters were counting on the University of Mississippi to help campaign. Ole Miss alumni were asked to return the favor for the support State graduates had given to Ole Miss alumni who had sought public office. For the first time, a Mississippi State graduate was seeking national office. According to one supporter, "This is one time that the Bulldogs of Mississippi State and the Rebels of Ole Miss can be together when we both can win."[26] A newly elected member of the Mississippi House and an Ole Miss law student, William Winter, campaigned for Stennis, rallying support for him on campus.[27] Winter briefly worked on Stennis's Washington staff. He remained active in Mississippi affairs, later serving as State Treasurer and Governor.

A letter-writing campaign also solicited votes for Stennis. Letters from Stennis's campaign office in Jackson detailed his platform, his qualifications, and the need to recruit for support. The state's newspapers published his platform. He appealed to the voters stating his support for agriculture based on his farm background. He cited his experience as a district attorney and judge, having been elected many times without opposition. He supported veterans. He condemned all outside interferences in the campaign. He clarified his position on: peace, roads, labor, education, health, old age assistance, taxes, and states' rights. He supported the United Nations as a means to facilitate world peace. He promised to help construct an all-weather, farm-to-market road system. He upheld both management and labor, provided they did not harm the public. He planned to secure federal funds for education but emphatically stated that the control of those funds would remain with state and local governments. He was not in favor of socialized medicine but would support assistance to those in need. He wanted to raise the income tax exemption and institute joint returns for married couples.

On the issue of states' rights he stated, "I am opposed to and will fight to the finish any attempt [by] Washington to inflict upon our people any legislation or regulation that conflicts with such rights."[28] States' rights statements were as close as Stennis came to addressing the race issue. For the white voters, who, in reality, were the only voters, this meant maintaining the status quo in race relations. Keeping on the high ground, he refrained from personally attacking his opponents.

While some newspapers were slow in supporting Stennis, a few promoted him immediately after the announcement. The *Webster Progress* endorsed Stennis early in the campaign with the following statement:

> We may be pardoned for expressing our delight that such an estimable gentleman is entering the lists and is a subject of choice for the highest office of the people of Mississippi. For we can declare that we know of no man within the borders of our great state whether a candidate therefore or not, more eminently fitted for the role of the United States Senator than Judge Stennis. Endowed with long years of experience as a public servant, as a legislator, prosecutor, and on the bench, [he possesses] a highly developed sense of responsibility, abundant common sense, a spotless record of deportment as both an individual and official, and a shining Christian character. Judge Stennis's candidacy should no doubt make special appeal to those who would be inclined to place the highest type of man in our most important office. Astute student of international affairs, talented in public speech, polished in manners, deferential and courteous, but very firm in his convictions, man of culture, a scholar and a gentleman, Judge Stennis could bring much dignity and power to the office of United States Senator.[29]

In the candidate's judicial district, Starkville's *News* broke its election neutrality rule on September 14, 1947, "Judge Stennis has shown a high sense of responsibility, abundant common sense, clean character, and outstanding leadership. His record is clean and above board and there can be no blasphemy directed toward him in the forthcoming political campaign."[30]

To get his message to the citizens, Stennis embarked on a state-wide tour to win votes making speeches on the courthouse steps. Stennis's official opening speech was held in Meridian on September 18. Followers from all over the state were invited there to demonstrate that a multitude supported his candidacy. Then to Vicksburg before heading north through the Delta, northeast Mississippi, and back to the Jackson area. Along the way he obtained the names of a large number of potential workers who could organize Stennis Clubs in each county.[31] Customarily, he would present his platform and be interrupted several times by applause. Stennis promised to "launch and keep this campaign on a high and lofty plane—come what will. I shall go right down the middle of the road in a hard, clean fight for sound, progressive, constructive government."[32] The conclusion of his first speech became the Stennis Creed.

> I want to go to Washington as the free and unfettered servant of the great body of the people who actually carry the burden of everyday life. I want to go there with directions from the people to pass on all matters affecting any group, or any interest, with fairness to all, and with a view to the public good. This is the course I have followed during my twenty years as an elected servant of the people, and it is on this basis alone that I want to represent you in the United States Senate. I want to plow a straight furrow right down to the end of my row. This is my political religion, and I have lived by it too long to abandon it now. I base my campaign on this statement, and with it I shall rise or fall.[33]

The speech, carried by radio stations in Meridian, Columbus, Tupelo, and Clarksdale, was financed by the Lowndes County Stennis Committee. Stennis traveled the state for the next month and a half. He presented his ideas without bands and other fanfare, marking a stark departure from Bilbo's theatrics. Bilbo's typical production included a country band to entertain the crowd followed by a fiery speech punctuated with vitriolic racial slurs. In contrast, Stennis probably was dull. His platform was devoid of any racial epithets. He did not tell jokes or stories, but only emphasized it was "time for a new day in Mississippi politics."[34] At 46 he told the listeners he was young enough to have the energy for the tremendous task of being a U. S. Senator and old enough to use his experience as a former state legislator, district attorney, and circuit judge in making important decisions.

After analyzing his speeches for a research project, Mississippi State Professor Mary Dazey concluded that Stennis:

> Had broad flexible style, which he can adjust to appeal to a wide variety of audiences on many occasions and still remain consistent to his own perceptions of the form of the public address and the role of the public speaker. The total absence of humor, his selections of subjects, and his detached, objective approach, suggests that he perceives of the public address as serious, formal, and didactic and the role of the speaker is that of a moral and spiritual individual speaking without passion or histrionics on subjects that are of vital concern to his audiences.[35]

His son, John Hampton, often accompanied his father on the road. According to him, his father would insert a few lines on local issues, but otherwise the speech was basically the same for all counties. He never called any of his opponents by name, except John Rankin, whom he credited with supporting TVA. John Hampton enjoyed riding in the sound truck as it cruised through the communities announcing the time and place for the next campaign speech. Although he would travel with his father only a couple of days a week, John Hampton memorized his father's speech.

In those days, lacking television and other social activities, people would come to hear political candidates in person. Poor roads, old cars, and Stennis's ulcer made the campaign trail grueling. With a short campaign period and the whole state to cover, they had little time between stops to eat. For a quick meal, Stennis carried milk and crackers in a black briefcase. He would leave DeKalb early on Monday mornings and return Saturday nights. His driver was a cousin, James Howell Stennis, who took a leave of absence as a Mississippi Highway Safety Patrolman to help with the Stennis campaign. Known by most as "Tuff" Stennis, he was informed by the higher authorities in the Patrol that he would not be reinstated if he quit to drive the candidate His immense respect for Stennis made accepting the job a given, especially when Stennis refused to take "no" for an answer. After the election, Tuff returned to the Patrol, the earlier admonition conveniently forgotten.

Tuff praised Stennis as "a twenty-four hour man who liked people… He had time for anybody, rich or poor, black or white."

They rented a Chevrolet for campaign travel over the mostly gravel and dirt roads of rural Mississippi. Once, Stennis chided his cousin for running a stop sign near Brooksville, "I knew you would make a mistake."

Tuff recalled one muddy trip to Liberty for a speech when only one man riding a mule showed. Stennis delivered his entire speech "word for word" to that one man.

As they traveled the state, the people who came to see and hear Stennis may have expected a private conversation, but he insisted that his cousin remain by his side. He had nothing to hide and would not be making any behind-the-scene promises in order to gain a vote. After the election, railroad men came to contribute to the campaign, but Stennis refused to accept their contributions.[36] Another cousin, Jesse Stennis, district attorney in Noxubee County, canvassed North Mississippi for votes, while the candidate's brother-in-law, Irvin Jones, is credited with carrying Perry County. One Jackson supporter remarked, "I don't believe I ever saw a man with as many kinfolk as John Stennis."[37]

While most were inexperienced in political campaigns, his friends were hard workers. He acknowledged their efforts, "I found that a person with his heart in the work and with a zeal and determination to work for you is worth a hundred of the other kind and will be able to do more even if he is inexperienced."[38] As a circuit judge, he was well known in his district, which included the counties of Clay, Kemper, Lowndes, Oktibbeha, and Noxubee. Fellow judge and supporter J.P. Coleman often arranged for Stennis to hold court in his district so he would be better known there. Stennis relied on the county courthouses for support.

Stennis was known in other parts of the state for making speeches supporting the United Nations. World War II had just ended. Stennis believed the new organization represented a means of finding peaceful solutions to the world's problems.

Unlike Rankin and Colmer, who had connections to Washington, Stennis could not be blamed for national problems. Those working for his election would often present this theme when soliciting votes.

As the time for the election neared, many voters did not appear to be interested in the Senate race. The crowds coming to the political rallies dwindled. In one instance Sam Wilhite reported that Stennis was speaking "to one black man and a telephone post. In fact, the people inside the courthouse didn't even bother to come out."[39]

Stennis kept his speeches on a high plane, as he had promised. He stayed with his platform—no "mudslinging" toward the other candidates. Long after the election, Stennis and Rankin remained friends. After being in Washington a couple of years, Stennis wrote Rankin, "Mrs. Stennis and I both greatly appreciate your friendship and the fine associations we have had with you in Washington, and we appreciate sharing with you membership in the Mississippi Congressional delegation. You have been most generous with us."[40]

Eventually, the state's newspapers took a more active part in the campaign. Ironically, the Tupelo *Daily Journal* endorsed Stennis over its hometown candidate, John Rankin. Rankin had been instrumental in making Tupelo the first city to be served by TVA. Yet, the *Journal* failed to endorse him. According to the editor, George McLean, he had not met anyone acquainted with Stennis who "did not speak in the highest terms of his Christian character, his fair-mindedness, and his ability."[41] Other newspapers attacked Rankin's playing up "racial and sectional hatreds" in the campaign.

Forest Jackson called himself the "heir of Bilbo," and criticized Stennis's and Colmers's records of public service.[42]

Colmer had the support of the Jackson *Daily News* but not the Biloxi-Gulfport *Daily Herald*, which remained neutral. He also won the support of Delta planters and politicians, as well as endorsement of the Rosedale *Bolivar County Times*. The out-of-state Memphis *Commercial Appeal*, a widely read newspaper in the Delta region, was targeted, however, for interference in Mississippi's affairs. The Delta vote was critical in winning the election. Colmer failed to receive the endorsement of Sharkey County's Governor Fielding Wright, a Delta resident, who remained neutral. The majority of Wright's previous campaign staff supported Stennis.

The state's largest paper, the Jackson *Clarion Ledger*, continued to support Paul Johnson while Johnson's hometown paper, the Hattiesburg *American*, maintained its neutral stance. As election time approached, some newspapers reported that Stennis appeared to have a slight edge on Colmer, followed by Jackson, Johnson, and Rankin. L.R. Collins running on the Republican ticket received little attention from the state's press.[43] Both the *New York Times* and *Time* magazine narrowed the election to a choice between Stennis and Colmer.

Stennis continued speaking across the state. On Monday, October 27, he held a rally in Jackson's Poindexter Park. To ensure a large crowd, Morrow promoted a forty-county drive-in, directing them to all arrive at the same time, so that traffic jams would focus media attention on the large number attending the event. It worked.[44]

In Fulton on Friday, October 31, Stennis predicted victory. During his final speech in Baldwyn on Saturday night, November 1, he summarized his campaign:

> When this campaign began we had $1,000, some loyal friends and a lot of hope. Since that time the friends have grown in numbers, and it is their splendid work that has brought us to this point where victory is in sight. We have been able to bring our message to most of the people of the state, and they are responding because they believe that a man fresh from the people can build a career of service for Mississippi in the Senate. It was my pledge when this campaign was opened that we would keep it on a high plane and wage a hard fight right down to the end. We have kept

the faith, and I am humbly proud of the fight that has been made in my behalf by thousands of good citizens all over the state.[45]

After a state-wide "live" speech on the radio from Hattiesburg November 3, Stennis concluded his campaign for the U. S. Senate. Most of the state's newspapers had encouraged the voters to come to the polls, especially since it was a plurality election. While Morrow predicted Stennis would win by a large margin, most political observers believed the margin would be small. As the results began coming in, Stennis took the lead. The Kemper County's two boxes of returns came in before the polls closed because all the registered voters had voted. Although his numbers were challenged throughout the night, he never lost that margin. His three-thousand-vote lead increased the next day as final ballots were counted. With all but about a hundred precincts in, he led ahead by almost six thousand votes, carrying thirty-seven of the state's eighty-two counties. When the victory was evident, Stennis thanked his supporters.

> I shall be eternally grateful for the vote of confidence which was given me by the good people of Mississippi. My election came as the direct result of individual efforts of hundreds of friends, both old and new, in every section of the state. I shall dedicate my service in the Senate to the goal of measuring up to this splendid confidence which has been shown in me by these friends, and especially by my neighbors in Kemper and the surrounding counties. I shall go to the Senate without obligations or commitments save to serve the plain people of Mississippi. We made this campaign without factionalism or partisanship, and I shall feel free to act as the unfettered servant of all people.[46]

The Jackson *Daily News*, a Colmer supporter, conceded, "We bow to the will of the majority and extend to Senator Stennis our congratulations and good wishes."[47] The *Webster Progress*, an avid Stennis supporter, reported, "Circuit Judge John C. Stennis, 46 year old liberal conservative, who refused to engage in either labor or racial controversies during his campaign and who refrained from criticizing his five opponents, was elected United

States Senator in Tuesday's election."[48] *Time* reported that after the Mississippi electorate had given "ranting" John Rankin, "the last of the notorious demagogues... the "worst beating of his career," they elected Stennis, who "was spare and scholarly....In him Mississippians hoped they had a man who would return to the hard working senatorial traditions of Pat Harrison and John Sharp Williams."[49]

John C. Stennis was now ready to embark on his career as a U. S. Senator alongside Senator James Eastland.

Eastland was no stranger to Stennis as they both served in the Mississippi legislature during Governor Theodore G. Bilbo's second term. Eastland had remained neutral during the race, stating that he would work with whomever Mississippians elected. Someone in Washington asked Eastland, "How did that fellow get in down there?

Eastland replied, "Well, while they were down there arguing about who would make the race and what could be done, Stennis and his crowd were at work. He got in the lead and they didn't overtake him."[50]

After the election Stennis named Bob Morrow as his administrative assistant, and Frank Smith agreed to serve on his staff. They left immediately after the election to organize Stennis's Washington office. After observing the women typing campaign literature in the Jackson headquarters, Smith suggested that Stennis hire Lorraine Lowery. She later became Stennis's personal secretary.[51] During the election, Morrow told Stennis he would take care of any necessary promises for political favors. When the election was over, he handed Stennis a piece of paper saying that the promises were on the other side. When Stennis turned the page over, it was blank. Morrow's only request was that Stennis take care of veterans.

On November 17, 1947, Senator Eastland reported the death of Senator Bilbo by presenting a resolution expressing sympathy for his death and asking that the Senate's sympathy be extended to his family. Also, "That as a further mark of respect to the memory of the deceased, the Senate, at the conclusion of its business, do adjourn."[52]

Following that announcement, Senator Eastland presented the credentials of John C. Stennis from Governor Fielding L. Wright, declaring that he had been duly elected by the qualified electors of Mississippi. After accepting the credentials, President Pro Tempore, Arthur H. Vandenberg administered to Stennis the oath of office.[53] Mississippians in Washington witnessed this historic event.

The Stennis family accompanied him to Washington on the train from Mississippi. In addition to his wife and children, John Hampton and Margaret Jane, his two sisters, Janie and Bessie, along with his oldest brother Sam from Pampa, Texas, made the trip. According to John Hampton, Mr. Prichard from Oktibbeha, Mr. Mosley and Mr. Slaughter from the hotel in Columbus, and Mr. Warren from DeKalb also were there.

J.P. Coleman joined the others as well, "I saw him take the oath of allegiance as the U. S. Senator ... and left Washington and came home with a feeling that it didn't make much difference about what might happen hereafter in political history, particularly in reference to myself. We had already been guilty of a major accomplishment."[54]

It would be pure speculation to consider the outcome of the election had a run-off been held. Many agree that Colmer would have had the advantage when Johnson, who split the south Mississippi vote, was out of the race. A run-off would also have given Colmer more time to campaign. In addition, other candidates might have thrown their support to him. Coleman's conclusion that they had pulled off a major victory provided John C. Stennis the opportunity to prove himself in his next great challenge, the United States Senate. Winning the election was certainly a major triumph.

Stennis with daughter, Margaret Jane, and son, John Hampton, and wife,
Coy, after being sworn into the U. S. Senate in 1947.
(Courtesy Kemper County Historical Association)

CHAPTER III
FIRST YEARS IN THE SENATE

The fast paced life in metropolitan Washington, DC was far different from what the Stennis family knew in DeKalb. Even the dial telephone was new to Coy Stennis, as an operator assisted calls in DeKalb. John Hampton told of counting the bridges they passed in order to remember how to get to the Rock Creek Parkway and their house on Brandywine Street. Their first house in Washington was a modest three bedroom two bath home. John Hampton and his sister, Margaret Jane, attended Alice Deal Junior High School and later Woodrow Wilson Senior High School. Both children adapted well to their new schools and did not fall behind.[1]

Stennis complained to those back home about the lack of good cornbread in Washington. According to his DeKalb secretary, Bobbie Harbour, Stennis stayed in Washington to accomplish the job Mississippians had sent him to do, but he always considered DeKalb to be home.[2]

Focused on his new responsibilities in the Senate, Stennis arrived ready to work and eager to learn. He commented, "I'm willing to start at the bottom and work my way up."[3] He didn't want to "pop-off." He promised to work with Senator Eastland and the rest of the Mississippi delegation for the good of the state, which was something Bilbo had not always done.

Stennis was assigned a seat on the Public Works Committee and the Committee on Rules and Administration. Given his interest in boosting Mississippi agriculture, he had wanted to serve on the Agriculture Committee, but senior Senator Eastland had his eyes on that committee. The Eastland family had a large farm in the Mississippi Delta. Whereas Stennis's committee assignments were not considered the most important, he believed he could help Mississippi on the Public Works Committee. His first legislative initiative was a federal program to pave rural roads and get Mississippi farmers "out of the mud." Early in his Senate career he introduced a bill known as the "State-Aid Program" that made county roads eligible for federal funds.[4] Electricity and telephone service were luxuries unavailable to many home state residents. Remembering the lack of health care for Mississippians during World War II due to a shortage of doctors and facilities, Stennis also strongly supported the National Hospital Program.[5]

After hearing complaints from Mississippi cotton farmers about allotment reductions, Stennis explained that surplus cotton supplies should be reduced. When informed that cotton acreage was lower than it was in 1871, Stennis introduced legislation that would halt future reductions and even add 100,000 acres for the under-four-acre farmers.[6]

Although he could not gain a seat on the Agriculture Committee with Eastland, he did become a member of the so called "Senate Club," which had excluded his predecessor Bilbo and current Senator Eastland as well. While some in "The Club" deny its existence, most agree that it is composed of those senators who respect the institution of the Senate and are not using it as a stepping stone to the presidency. One in "The Club" described one member as: "His head swims with its [the Senate's] history, its love and the accounts of past personal deeds and purposes. To him precedent has almost a mystical meaning."[7]

The Southern Democrats had a hold on the Senate since they were usually re-elected without opposition and, with their tenure, occupied the chairmanships of important committees. One powerful democratic senator, Richard Russell from Georgia, served on both the Armed Services and the Appropriations Committees. Russell, a member of "The Club," took an interest in the new senator from Mississippi, quickly becoming his mentor and friend. Stennis adopted Russell's senatorial strategies. Russell wanted to be "a workhorse rather than a show horse" by working silently behind the scenes. Russell did not get involved in an issue until a national level of concern developed. Always well informed, he had little patience with other senators who did not have full knowledge of the legislation before the Senate. Even before becoming a senator, Stennis was always well informed before he made any official statements.

By working within the inner circle of the Senate, Russell became a "senator's senator" and was considered "most influential." Russell's successful Senate career could be attributed to "his integrity, his fairness, his willingness to accommodate colleagues when possible, and his practice of maintaining confidences."[8] According to Stennis, "You always knew where he stood, without his running out front."[9]

Russell could not get Stennis on Appropriations but was able to place him on a sub-committee of the Armed Services Committee.[10] When Stennis received word of this appointment he responded, "You understand I am no committee hog and I am not trying to push anyone else out and if I am not the one to serve in this capacity, I want you to be free to say so."[11]

Before the appointment, Stennis had asked those with knowledge about the Korean War to share unclassified information with him. He told the Senate that his constituents were asking questions for which he had no answers. Knowing that he would have to explain to Mississippians should the war effort seriously deteriorate, he wanted information, "I certainly am not a military man and I am not seeking to offer military advice; but from such light as I have before me, I think that the day has long since arrived when we ought to strike communist China with all of the force and power that we have; we ought to give the commander in Korea full power to strike with everything we have, in every way he can and I urge that we either strike in this manner or that we evacuate and get out of Korea."[12] Stennis's philosophy to strike with all of the force necessary to win the war or quit was set, and this plea would be reiterated several times in future military actions. Following his appointment to the Military Preparedness Investigation Sub-Committee in January 1951, he would have access to military information.

In addition to military information, Stennis's subsequent position on the Armed Services Committee gave him the opportunity to improve military facilities in Mississippi. He was responsible for locating the Meridian Naval Air Station in Mississippi in 1957. The station had been scheduled to be constructed in Louisiana. When a constituent informed Stennis of that news, he was able to convince the Navy to locate it in Mississippi.

The construction of the Meridian base required citizens to give up land that had been in their families for over a century. Stennis wanted to talk with the landowners to explain the importance of the Naval Air Station. When discussing what type of speaker's platform would be needed for the speech, he said all he needed was a pick-up truck.[13]

Stennis strongly supported Columbus Air Force Base and Greenville Air Force Base, as well as Keesler Air Force Base at Biloxi, for both their military significance and the jobs they provided for local citizens. When the Defense Department planned to close the Greenville Air Force Base in 1962, Stennis told a constituent, "Confidentially, when they sent the man over here to announce to me the tentative decision to deactivate the Base, I gave back some strong language and appealed directly to the Secretary of Defense. I shall tell the rest of it when we see each other."[14] Stennis's influence gave the base a few years, but it closed in 1965 and was given to the City of Greenville.

Stennis valued the U. S. Army's Camp Shelby near Hattiesburg as well. He wanted to make the operation, "one of the largest and most suitable National Guard training sites in the nation."[15] He always believed that a strong military would cause the Russians to think twice before attacking the United States. Stennis also helped Mississippi military contractors secure sizable contracts. Senator Margaret Chase Smith wondered why her state, Maine, could not get a few of the Navy shipbuilding contracts awarded instead to Ingalls in Pascagoula.

Stennis did not spend all of his time working. He enjoyed "fact finding," as well as hunting trips with his desk mate, Willis Robertson from Virginia. Stennis noted to Robertson, "You are on the Appropriation Committee and I am on the Armed Services Committee and we can therefore get most any trip which we should desire, at least through the year 1952. Such possibilities may be questionable thereafter...why not set up travel targets for 1951 and 1952 to take advantage of the opportunity?"[16]

One plan Robertson envisioned called for an overseas visit to inspect oil activities, Communist infiltration, territorial government, foreign aid, and rearmament in India, Pakistan, Saudi Arabia, Iran, Turkey, Italy, France, and Germany. While abroad Robertson suggested "partridge, Chokkar [chukar], and dear [deer] hunts" as well as duck, woodcock, and wild boar and possibly a tiger or leopard hunt. In addition to the hunting, he mentioned for Christmas presents that they could buy china, fine table linen and banquet cloths as well as silk lingerie.[17]

To repay Robertson for invitations to hunt with him in Virginia, Stennis wanted him to come to Mississippi. After a visit to Jackson they could go fishing in the Gulf. Stennis thought he could get the Air Force to provide transportation to Biloxi. Later Stennis was criticized for extravagance in traveling at the government's expense. Even though it would be against his nature to be extravagant, Stennis clearly took advantage of traveling overseas early in his Senate career.

While he made no comments about race in his campaign, fighting civil rights legislation quickly dominated Stennis's time and energy. Truman's Civil Rights Committee recommended a permanent Fair Employment Practices Committee (FEPC), desegregation of the armed forces, and adoption of other measures to reduce discrimination. To Mississippians, accepting these civil rights measures by Congress would mean an end to the southern way of life.

Stennis was still learning how to be a senator. He acknowledges that even though a freshman, "he should listen more and talk less. But freshman or no, I do not intend to sit idly by and see Mississippi and other Southern states' traditions and institutions destroyed by those outsiders who wish to enhance their own political fortunes at our expense."[18]

Shortly after his election Stennis received a letter with a different view, "If you will be as radical for all the peoples' rights, regardless of race, creed, or color I would think that you would go down in history as one of the greatest statesmen from the Southern states. I am a white man, and I badly differed with the late Bilbo's philosophy. I hope you will take this letter in the spirit it is written."[19]

Stennis thanked the writer for his concern, but chose not to follow his advice. The majority of letters Stennis received were against civil rights legislation. When he was accused of being lukewarm in opposing civil rights he replied, "You can be sure that I will join with other Southern leaders to withstand any attempts to dictate changes in our way of life."[20]

Most of his replies were more diplomatic. He simply wrote, "These are difficult times." He realized that the fight to maintain the status quo would be a long battle. He answered a Vicksburg writer, "It is too bad that we may have to spend our energies in a fight over so-called civil rights when there are so many grave dangers confronting us from all over the world."[21]

Stennis received some observations from Senator Dennis Chavez, a sixteen year veteran from New Mexico, "Young man, they [the other senators] treat you pretty nice here, but they do not give you a darn thing."[22] Stennis, however, quickly gained their respect. He knew the South was targeted by senators from the rest of the country for its segregation policies. Stennis wanted to tell the South's side of the issue.

In spite of his promise to maintain the status quo, some Mississippians, accustomed to the demagoguery of Bilbo, continued to accuse Stennis of not fighting hard enough against civil rights legislation. Stennis believed that divisive press releases only strengthened the resolve of those supporting civil rights legislation. To one supporter he replied:

> Now, it is my opinion that a man can do more by a process of personal reasoning with the men who are going to pass on those matters here, or at least I decidedly feel that I can do more that way, than by issuing a lot of statements to the press. We must remember that it is not the people of Mississippi who are going to decide on these matters, because all of us see it the same way.[23]

The southern group opposed all of the FEPC directives by claiming "state's rights." To prevent civil rights legislation from being introduced, Southern senators who held committee chairmanships through seniority merely ignored the proposals. When legislation succeeded in getting to the Senate for a vote, they resorted to filibusters. The FEPC legislation targeted job discrimination, lynching and poll taxes. Many southern states, like Mississippi, required voters to pay an annual tax in order to vote as a means to prevent poorer blacks from voting. In addition to the poll tax, Mississippi required registered voters to be capable of interpreting parts of the Mississippi Constitution. Since many blacks were not educated, satisfying this requirement was often difficult.

On March 4, 1948, Stennis was recognized for his first speech in the Senate against the anti-poll tax legislation. It was unusual for a new Senator to make a major speech so early in his career, but Senator Russell, his well-respected friend, gave him the opportunity. In this speech Stennis defended the rights of states to establish voting requirements because that right was reserved for the states, not being specifically covered in the Constitution. He proclaimed that interest groups were "destroying the Constitution," that much of the push for civil rights legislation was political. Stennis insisted on committee hearings before legislation; none had been held since 1943 on the anti-poll tax legislation. In addition, Stennis complained that the subcommittee, which sent the bill to the floor, did not have southern representation. The South would solve the racial problem in its own way, under its own timetable, and much more effectively without outside interference.

After this speech, Senator Burnet Maybank of South Carolina said that Stennis gave, "one of the greatest and most statesman like speeches that has been made for many a year."[24]

Upon Stennis's recommendation, hearings were held on the anti-poll tax bill. But the bill remained alive.

In July of 1948 Stennis prepared to lead the filibuster effort against the anti-poll tax legislation. While Stennis was not opposed to submitting a constitutional amendment to ban the poll tax, he would be against its ratification. Stennis believed that if the federal government could pass this legislation, the next step would be to establish voter qualifications. In his opinion the Constitution was going to be repealed "bit by bit."

Speaking of blacks, Stennis said, "We have taken the most backward people from the world's darkest continent, and in a little more than a century, we have trained them, given them a religion, given them an education, given them the rights of citizenship, protected these rights in and out of court and, to a certain degree, given them a culture."[25] Stennis strongly believed that blacks owed their presence here to the white race and should be appreciative enough to remain subservient. In general, southern leaders believed that "separate but equal" treatment of blacks was working satisfactorily, and that northern leaders who were pushing civil rights legislation did not fully understand the relationship between blacks and whites in the South. The schools were not equal, and Stennis knew that black schools must be improved in order to maintain segregation. In a memo he wrote, "Should segregation be declared unlawful, we must find some method to continue our public schools under conditions that will preserve the identity of the races." Possibly, if those outside the South knew what progress was being made, they would be less judgmental.

During the summer of 1949, Stennis joined Senators Richard Russell from Georgia and Harry Byrd of Virginia in leading another filibuster against the anti-poll tax legislation. Sounding the "states' rights" mantra, Stennis declared that based on the Constitution, determining voter qualifications was the responsibility of the states. An amendment would be necessary to remove the poll tax.

Civil rights supporters in Congress, along with President Truman, knew that the filibuster would be used against any civil rights legislation. To halt filibustering, northern senators wanted to invoke a cloture rule to limit debate by the vote of a simple majority. Southern senators vehemently objected. Their leader, Richard Russell, stated that the Senate "stood as the last citadel of free and full discussion where the rights of the minority can be heard and fully protected."[26] The attempt to limit debate was defeated by the southern senators who gained a slight victory by requiring that a two-thirds vote of all senators, rather than just those present when a vote was taken, would be necessary to halt debate.

Stennis had the respect of northern senators even though they disagreed on civil rights issues. Concerned Senator Alexander Smith representing Rhode Island wrote him, "I am thinking of a get-together…without benefit of press, or any other publicity media, where I could present to you more fully my own thinking…and in return you could explain to me…why there seem to be roadblocks to any form of legislation that might be classified under the general heading of civil rights."[27]

To help "educate" those not familiar with southern traditions, Stennis requested that the governors of the Southern states send him information on what they were doing to improve the plight of blacks in their state. The condensed information was published by *Colliers* in a March 1949 article entitled, "What You Don't Know About the South." Stennis highlighted progress in education, health services, and land ownership. Acknowledging that much more needed to be done, Stennis asked the rest of the nation for:

> Understanding of our problem and adequate recognition of the progressive accomplishments. These accomplishments have been no easy matter in a region still burdened by excessive poverty. But we are confident that when our nation as a whole understands our real problem and learns what we have already accomplished, we will have new and sympathetic co-operation as we go on to remove the remaining obstacles to our progress.[28]

While Stennis may have been sincere in demonstrating success in solving the problems of the South, civil rights supporters were not convinced and introduced an anti-lynching bill.

Stennis told the Senate Judiciary Subcommittee that lynching was almost eliminated in the South, with Mississippi having only one case in 1947. He attributed the reduction to increased local involvement in attacking the crime. He argued that with the reduction in lynching, cooperation between races in the South had improved. Given the proposed law's unconstitutionality, an anti-lynching law was not necessary. Stennis stated that the South is wary of "the crank, the outside meddler and the paid agitators who make their living by stirring up strife and enmity among the races, there and elsewhere." Comparing the new legislation with Reconstruction rules, he advised, "Do not afflict the races with such an artificial and unnecessary burden again."[29]

After a six day filibuster on the anti-lynching bill, the anti-lynching supporters gave up.[30] Stennis never advocated or supported violence or the breaking of the law, but steadfastly maintained that the South could and would protect the civil rights of all of its citizens.

The push for civil rights among blacks was not universal. Some were satisfied with the current situation and did not favor outside influences. They may have said this in order to remain in good graces with the white community. Their comments created confusion, divided the cause, and gave those opposed to civil rights more ammunition to resist change. Violence against blacks continued.

With the 1948 presidential election looming, the black vote was critical to Truman's re-election. While part of his support for civil rights legislation could be political, he was very concerned about treatment of southern blacks. Southern Democrats told Truman they could not support him if he continued to push civil rights legislation. Notwithstanding his Confederate ancestry and Missouri upbringing, Truman told them, "But my very stomach turned over when I learned that Negro soldiers just back from overseas were being dumped out of army trucks in Mississippi and beaten. Whatever my inclinations as a native of Missouri might have been, as President I know this is bad. I shall fight to end evils like this."[31]

Stennis received a poignant letter in 1944 from a Kemper County soldier during World War II. Its message was prophetic, but unheeded by Stennis:

> Well the question is and what seems to be confusing the most of us is the Negro situation. You see I am in a position to know that the Negro situation is going to be a problem and it is not going to be easily solved. You see we are in this war together the North-South-East and West—and

you know that the Negroes are with us as well as the white. And after this war they are going to want the same treatment as we get. And the reason for that is, well you know the little Negro that we once avoided, well that little boy is playing a big part in this war. You see when you are in a dirty, muddy foxhole you are not particular if he is black or white as long as he is ther[e] to help you when you need him most. Now are we going to play the game with them now and after the war ignore them.[?] Well, the reason for asking you this question, you see, I am with a gang of boys from the North as well as the South. And that is our biggest argument that we can find to pass the time away. In other word[s] we fight the Civil War more than we do this one."[32]

Southern senators continued to resist every effort by the administration and those in Congress to support civil rights. John Stennis along with his mentor, Richard Russell of Georgia, led the Southern delegation in attempts to defeat any legislation that required changing the southern way of life. Teams were formed to prevent a quick move by the opposition to pass civil rights legislation. Stennis once rushed for a possible vote still wearing his pajamas. One of the group remained on the Senate floor any time the Senate was in session. The majority of Southern Democrats vowed not to support their party's platform.

Stennis, however, stayed with the Democratic Party in spite of President Truman's position. Stennis gave Truman high marks among the presidents who served with him. He said Truman "overcame his supposed lack of education. He was a wild mule when it came to learning things that he was interested in....He had a rugged honesty that made him very effective."[33] Holding this attribute close to his own character, Stennis respected honesty in others.

The Southern Democrats tried to get Truman not to run for re-election. They wanted to weaken his civil rights platform, but when that effort failed at the Democratic Convention held in Philadelphia July 12, 1948, they nominated Richard Russell for president. Russell received 263 votes to Truman's 947.5 votes. Stennis, one of the first to support Russell, declared, "I was for him all the way to Victory."[34] According to Stennis, "Senator Russell is one

Stennis (far right) respected Truman for his tenacity and his willingness to learn more about a problem before making a decision. He commented that Truman made the momentous decision to drop the atom bomb, thereby changing the world's view of war in the future. (Courtesy Kemper County Historical Association)

of my great favorites in the Senate, and I can really say that he is my top favorite. He represents a rare combination of learning, ability, coolness, modesty, and unselfishness that you seldom find in one personality. ...He is the most valuable man to the South in the entire Senate."[35]

Stennis was also a valuable man in the Senate. Often, he was called on to preside in the absence of the Vice President and he "set a record for getting business transacted. He uses the same decorum learned as a circuit court judge, where he picks up the gavel and gets down to action without a lot of noise from either the galleries or from the Senate floor."[36]

While southern senators would have to continue their vigilance on civil rights with Truman's victory, a democratic majority in the Senate allowed them to regain committee chairmanships. Events other than civil rights required the Senate's attention.

The Cold War

Stennis told Mississippi Farm Bureau members at their annual meeting in Jackson in 1948 that he did not believe the Russians would attack, because of "the passage of our selective service act, our newly created seventy group Air Force, the Marshall Plan, and the atomic bomb."[37] When campaigning in 1947, Stennis championed the United Nations as the world court. As a judge he had confidence in it and hoped that international conflicts could be resolved without war. Stennis predicted that if "war is staved off for the next 20 to 25 years, the world will move into the greatest era of peace, progress, and creative building the world has ever known."[38] However, Russia was not interested in world peace. In spite of Stennis's assurances, "World Domination"—the goal of Russia and Communism—created apprehension and concern.

Stennis was not on the Armed Services Committee when the conflict in Korea erupted, but he was on the committee investigating General Douglas McArthur's dismissal by President Truman for disagreements with the Administration's policy in Korea. The committee heard nineteen days of testimony. McArthur testified for three days, defending his offensive actions for seeking a victory in Korea while ignoring the fact that he could have escalated the conflict into a world war with China. McArthur suggested that nuclear bombs should be dropped on Chinese cities.[39]

After his televised address to Congress, McArthur was immensely popular. So many letters supporting McArthur came to Stennis's office that he and his staff couldn't read them all. The public clamored for televising the hearings. When Senator Russell Long asked Stennis his opinion, fearing that secrets might be revealed, he replied, "Russell, sometimes you have to vote to save this country even if it's not popular."[40]

Going against public opinion, Stennis concluded that Truman was right in dismissing McArthur; only the president and Congress could declare war, not the generals. While Stennis wanted a strong defense, he believed strongly that the military should remain under civilian control even though he did not always agree with that control. Stennis supported Truman's entry into the Korean conflict, but he did feel no clear strategy had been established; and the efforts of commanders in the field were often hamstrung by Washington politicians.[41] While he did not agree with giving McArthur sole authority to attack China, Stennis said "We ought to strike communist China with all the force and power we have" to halt communist aggression.[42]

In spite of his apprehension of Communism, he believed that communist witch hunts which implicated innocent Americans should be discontinued.

Admonishment of Self-appointed Communist Hunter

The identification of communist infiltrators in the government during the early 1950s became an obsession of Senator Joseph McCarthy (R. Wisconsin). Many believed he overstepped his authority. McCarthy subpoenaed witnesses to testify about their activities before his Permanent Subcommittee on Investigations, a part of the Government Operations Committee. In the hearings McCarthy badgered the witnesses. Many declared their Fifth

Amendment rights to prevent being trapped by charges which lacked substantial evidence. He was not popular among other Senators, but he attracted supporters as he became more powerful, even feared. According to President Truman, he was, "a ballyhoo artist who has to cover up his shortcomings by wild charges."[43]

A committee was established to investigate McCarthy and his committee. Members of the committee were men selected for their judicial background and moderate political views. For the committee, Minority Leader Lyndon Johnson selected John Stennis, who appropriately fit the selection criteria. At the completion of the hearing, Stennis was the first democratic senator to speak out against McCarthy. He accused McCarthy of "spreading slush and slime" on the Senate. Stennis believed that unless the committee's activities were halted "something fine and good will have left the Senate." Margaret Chase Smith (D. Maine) recalls Stennis's tone in the accusatory speech as being "very cold and chilling." On December 2, 1954, the Senate censured McCarthy, thereby ending his reign as the "self-appointed communist hunter."

McCarthy's methods were rebuked, but Americans were still faced by Communism's expansive efforts. Stennis's belief was that "containment and internationalism" could thwart its spread.[44] His convictions were reflected by his vote on the Marshall Plan and by his support of the North Atlantic Treaty Organization (NATO). For economic and military assistance provided to foreign powers, he supported the Mutual Defense Assistance Act (MDAA).

Later that legislation would provide a basis for entering the Vietnam conflict.[45] Stennis summarized his views on Asia in a memo to his files:

> We shall make our worst mistake, and perhaps a fatal one, if we attempt to crush Communism in Asia with American manpower. The area is too great. The distance is too far. Our manpower is limited. From a military standpoint the only way free nations of the West can win in Asia over the years is for us to train and equip the native troops in friendly Asiatic countries. From a political standpoint the people of the countries in Asia

must in some way cultivate a desire for freedom and a will to fight for that freedom. We can help encourage this spirit, but we cannot create it.[46]

Beginnings of the Vietnam Conflict

At the end of World War II, the French reclaimed their colony, Vietnam, which had been occupied by the Japanese. However, many Vietnamese were tired of colonial rule and wanted independence. Their communist leader Ho Chi Minh, who was in Moscow during the war, declared their independence on September 2, 1945, in Hanoi's Ba Dihn Square. Warfare between the French and the independent movement broke out in 1946.

To preclude the spread of Communism in the area, the United States supported the French in the conflict.[47] The French accepted U. S. financial aid but refused advice. Eisenhower's election in 1952 brought a renewed effort to halt the spread of Communism. By employing the "domino theory," in which small countries, one after another, would succumb to Communism, the communists would control large areas. To combat this expansion, the U. S. continued giving the French financial aid to fight the insurgents in Vietnam. By early 1954, $2 billion had been supplied to the French government.[48]

Since Eisenhower was a Republican, Stennis was not in his close circle of advisors. After a fact-finding trip to Europe, Stennis and two other Senators met with the President. During that meeting Stennis "observed an overworked and overburdened man. At the same time, he is a man of decision and showed a very fine knowledge of European affairs."[49]

Stennis, now a junior member of the Armed Services Committee, became concerned with how far we would go to defend Indo-China from the communist threat. He feared the U. S. was tied to too many treaties and, at the same time, he was leery of limited military involvement. The French asked for planes and support personnel to maintain them. In response, President Eisenhower agreed to supply B-26s for the Vietnam government to combat communist-led insurgents. To train those who would maintain the planes, he sent two hundred Air Force mechanics.

Stennis immediately objected to Eisenhower's actions, stating that without support from France and other countries, this act could lead the United States into a conflict that could not be won. On the Senate floor February 9, 1954, Stennis stated: "Step by step, we are moving into this war in Indochina and I am afraid we will move to a point from which there will be no return. If we are going to send men to Indochina for the purpose of keeping airplanes on the firing line, it is only natural that we send along the pilots and the trigger men. It is the next logical step."[50] Stennis knew that if the support personnel were attacked, this would bring the U. S. into the conflict.

Following just such an attack on the base where the airmen were stationed but absent, Stennis warned the Senate again March 9, 1954: a choice would have to be made on whether to stay in Vietnam or come home.

Taking Stennis's advice, Eisenhower agreed to bring the mechanics back, but later sent replacements. The French, in a last ditch effort to defend Dienbienphu, requested more planes, more support. Secretary of State John Foster Dulles remarked that a unified effort would be required to bring about a French victory.[51]

Other countries, however, would not agree to enter the conflict.

In a meeting April 3, 1954, Congressional leaders recommended that the President not send U. S.-manned aircraft to defend the communist-surrounded outpost of Dienbienphu. The outpost fell May 7, 1954.[52]

Stennis objected to unilateral involvement, stating, "I do not believe that Congress would ever vote, or should vote, to have the United States go in on a unilateral basis. It would have to be a real united effort....To go in on a unilateral basis would be to go into a trap. It would be to send our men into a trap from which there could be no reasonable recovery and no chance for victory.[53]

In the Geneva Accords of 1954, Vietnam was divided at the seventeenth parallel into North Vietnam, ruled by the communists and South Vietnam under Bao Dai's direction.

*As a Democrat and relative newcomer, Stennis was not in Eisenhower's circle
of advisors. He did, however, convince Eisenhower to recall airplane mechanics accompanying planes sent to Vietnam after the French left. Stennis stressed
that if the American soldiers were attacked, this would bring the U. S. into a
conflict that could not be won. Eisenhower brought the
mechanics back but then sent additional ones later.
(Courtesy Kemper County Historical Association)*

The division did not bring peace.

The Southeast Asia Collective Defense Treaty, which was signed in 1954, created the Southeast Asia Treaty Organization (SEATO). Signatory nations included the U. S., Great Britain, France, Australia, New Zealand, Pakistan, Thailand, and the Philippines. However, as Stennis feared, it was only a paper pact.[54] Later, Vietnam, Cambodia, and Laos were added by protocol; the Geneva agreement did not allow them to directly participate. The treaty gave the administration legitimacy in providing unilateral support to SEATO. The U. S. took up the battle the French lost.[55] The U. S. supported Ngo Diem replacing the French government's Premier Bao Dai. Diem's rule was so oppressive, however, that many South Vietnamese joined the National Liberation Front or Viet Cong in a campaign to end his reign and reunite North and South Vietnam.

To keep informed, Stennis requested that his staff meet each morning to review the Washington papers, including editorials. They followed proceedings in the *Congressional Record*. They read clippings from Mississippi papers. Stennis also requested a list of all visitors, letters, and telegrams received in his Washington office, along with copies of all letters sent by his staff. Stennis was meticulous in garnering information. He requested to receive a copy of *The Commercial Appeal* as soon as it arrived. Stennis expected his staff to strive for perfection, "One of my chief accomplishments…is the fact that I have reached the point in my service where I now have the potential of having the best staff on Capitol Hill, a reality that will be reached within three or four months of experience as a team."[57] His staff in 1954 included Clyde Mathews, Charlie W. Jones, Annie W. Rice, Lorane Lowry, Eleanor Gay, Mary Walker Gatewood, Lucille Young, and Sarah Dawson.

In 1955, Stennis supported Admiral Byrd's Expedition Deepfreeze by expediting the funding through hearings and subsequent Senate passage of S-2078. For his help, Rear Admiral Richard E. Byrd, expedition leader wrote, "In my time, I've witnessed a lot of performances on Capitol Hill. But for the consideration and speed, the Senate's performance in the case of S-2078 was really outstanding."[58] This expedition supported the International Geophysical Year scientific research projects. Following his "Look Ahead" motto, Stennis supported research efforts. But when the Supreme Court struck down the ruling allowing separate but equal facilities, Stennis was afraid of the future implications of this action. He preferred to "Look Back"—keeping the past and fearing the future.

Impacts of *Brown vs. the Board of Education*

The integration of public schools was Stennis's major concern regarding civil rights legislation. In 1952 he wrote that he believed the "separate but equal" doctrine must remain. "In Mississippi we must further and substantially extend our present plan of equalization of equipment, services, and curricula for our Negro children. Should segregation be declared unlawful, we must find some method to continue our public schools under conditions that will preserve the identity of the races. This is not race prejudice; it is race preservation, something recognized and desired by the thinking members of each race."[59]

Equality of education in the schools of Mississippi was far from equitable. Mississippi was spending more on transporting white students than on education of blacks.[60] Stennis was convinced that the public education system in Mississippi and the South would be destroyed by integration. In a 1954 letter to President Eisenhower he suggested that the President solicit input from small groups in each southern state.

> I am convinced we have not yet made to you the strong and almost unanimous sentiment prevailing among the mothers and fathers of the South against forced integration of our schools. This applies to both white and colored parents. Nor have we made it clear to you what will be the ultimate and fatal consequences of enforced integration...The real issue at stake is the survival of our public schools. Schools originate and are sustained through the efforts of dedicated teachers. This support and dedication cannot exist with schools integrated by force.[61]

The South's "separate but equal" doctrine legitimizing a dual educational system was based on an 1896 Supreme Court decision in *Plessy vs. Ferguson*. On May 17, 1954, the Supreme Court overturned the separate but equal policies in *Brown vs. the Board of Education*. This monumental decision removed the legal basis that southern states were using to maintain segregated schools.

Stennis's fellow senator, James Eastland, suggested that Mississippi abolish its public school system rather than comply. Uncharacteristically, Stennis went against Eastland on this issue. He quickly sent a memo to Eastland stating that he would openly oppose any attempt to close Mississippi's public schools. He knew that, "In great areas in Mississippi the attitude of the people was that they were going to keep their public schools and by indirect methods they would also keep them separate."[62]

Initially, the southern senators attacked the Supreme Court ruling as being unconstitutional.

To plead their case against the Brown decision, Southern senators issued the *Declaration of Constitutional Principles*, on March 12, 1956. This document became known as the *Southern Manifesto*. Stennis, along with senators Richard Russell of Georgia and Sam Irvin from North Carolina, authored the paper. All of the southern senators except Al Gore and Estes Kefaufer from Tennessee and Lyndon Johnson from Texas signed the Manifesto. As majority leader, Johnson implied agreement, but due to his position, declined to sign. Richard Russell, the leader of the Southern Democrats, knew that Johnson's chances to run for the presidency would be eliminated if he signed it.

The document attacked the Supreme Court decision, calling it "a clear abuse of judicial power."[63] Stennis believed the Court was acting beyond its power, "Inexperienced judges, appointed on a political basis, by both the Democratic and Republican Administrations have given us a Supreme Court made up more of social engineers and self-styled crusaders than seasoned judges, learned in the law."[64]

In spite of the Supreme Court ruling, the southern states continued to thwart any integration attempts. The first showdown using federal troops to enforce the Supreme Court's decision came in Little Rock, Arkansas when President Eisenhower sent federal troops to Little Rock in 1957 to enforce court-ordered desegregation. He defended his actions to Stennis by saying that he was only carrying out court orders and not coming "to enforce or to advance any governmental policy respecting integration, desegregation, or segregation."[65] Stennis questioned the use of these federal troops in Little Rock, stating that Eisenhower "acted hastily, was badly advised, and reached unwarranted conclusions that set a tragic precedent to plague our nation for decades to come."[66] Stennis did not question the authority of the President to enforce the law, but he believed that federal marshals, rather than bayonet-armed soldiers, should have been used. There was no rebellion or insurrection. Using the military was too great a show of force. Realizing that the federal government might now use force to implement desegregation everywhere, southern leaders worked within the new law to slow the progress of integration.

Though they had seen what was done in Little Rock, most blacks in Mississippi were afraid to file suit to enter the all-white schools. To insure white control, the Citizens' Council was established in 1954. This Mississippi group used economic methods of intimidation to prevent blacks from filing suits to enter white schools. Those black leaders and whites who projected equality between the races either lost their jobs or found their businesses boycotted.

To back up the Citizens' Council, in 1956 the Mississippi legislature created the Sovereignty Commission. The Commission was charged with the duty of securing information on individuals and groups who supported the efforts of the federal government to end segregation. While Stennis belonged to neither the Citizen's Council nor the Sovereignty Commission, he would address either group when asked. Stennis believed that local leaders could maintain segregation without these organizations. In one address Stennis suggested the Governor be made a member of all school boards, using his authority to determine where students attended school using "logical" reasons, rather than race. He stated that "states certainly have the power to take action to protect the health, the safety, the welfare, the morals, and the harmonious relations of the community."[67] Stennis urged both races to be "constantly reminded that the path for development for all of us lies along the road of peaceful and harmonious relationships... that we [Stennis] are going to do our part in maintaining such a course."[68]

Stennis had heard stories from his grandmother, who withstood the Siege of Vicksburg during the Civil War. Some of his earliest patriotic memories were the Confederate memorial celebrations on the courthouse square in DeKalb when the old cannon was fired. He supplied the names of relatives who had fought in the Civil War for inscription on a memorial and helped to get it erected. Most white southerners had a loyalty to the South and naturally distrusted northern or "Yankee" interference in their affairs. Chapters of the United Daughters of the Confederacy and the Sons of Confederate Veterans could be found in most towns. They kept the history of the Civil War alive, albeit with a southern slant. While not as publicly evident, all knew that the Ku Klux Klan existed and would occasionally burn a cross to warn those sympathetic to the plight of blacks. Stennis never condoned the Klan or any violent acts, but like many Southerners, he did possess southern sympathies. He visited Gettysburg, where one of his relatives was killed in battle. The park manager there mentioned to Stennis that adjacent land with historical significance was planned for development. The senator was able to get appropriations to purchase the land, even though some of the landowners contacted their own senators to object.[69] In a letter to his friend and early supporter Ed Brunini in Vicksburg, Stennis wanted one hundred thousand dollars earmarked for Vicksburg National Military Park improvements.

In spite of the "Think Ahead" signs that he prominently displayed in his office, why did he oppose statehoods for both Alaska and Hawaii in the late 1950s? Stennis had visited European refugee camps and was against legislation allowing "these people" to come over here by the thousands, declaring, "That in spite of its virtues in the past, the melting pot no longer melts."[70]

Other Mississippi leaders shared his views on Hawaii. Former Representative John Rankin reported that someone he considered "fishy" was going about the state making speeches supporting Hawaii for statehood. Rankin suggested Stennis have a committee investigate him or, if not, set the FBI onto it. Both Stennis and Rankin feared the addition of other cultures and races might bring representatives who would align with civil rights advocates.

Southern Democrats knew civil rights would highlight the party's platform in Chicago's 1956 Democratic Convention. Some believed their delegates should walk out as a way of protesting the civil rights platform. Stennis, who declared to be fair, firm, and be quite on the other hand, declared:

> If you send me as a delegate, I shall go there with fighting clothes on, but I shall not go there looking for a walk-out. I know many would like for us to walk out, others would like to see us walk out. As for me, I am staying...for the sake of our homes, our children, and our bloodstream, let's stand together as one....Whatever differences we have, let's fight them out on the floor of this convention if it takes until midnight tonight, tomorrow night, or next Tuesday night.[71]

Stennis went to the convention with determination to preserve the southern way of life, but Stennis and the other Mississippi delegates got little of what they wanted. The democratic platform called for voting rights for minorities, as well as equal employment opportunities and school desegregation.

The Democratic nominees were soundly defeated in the November election by the Republican challengers, Dwight Eisenhower and Richard Nixon. Stennis remained loyal to the Democratic Party because "it is the only major party that has a major objective in the matters of the farm bill [and] the only major party that puts Southern Senators and Congressmen in responsible places of power."[72] Stennis himself enjoyed the power of his reputation and wisdom to influence their decisions.

CHAPTER IV
THE KENNEDY-JOHNSON YEARS

President John F. Kennedy was one of Stennis's favorites. He considered him the most intelligent of all presidents with whom he worked.[1] While they were very much apart on the school desegregation issue, Stennis supported Kennedy, who often sought his advice. Through all administrations Stennis usually deferred to the presidents, "makes no difference who he is, I would back those fellows on a lot of things."[2] According to Stennis, Kennedy had to rely on others' advice and judgment for his decisions, because he just couldn't know everything on an issue.

When Kennedy told the nation that the United States was going to the moon, Stennis was chairman of the Appropriation Subcommittee on Space. According to Stennis, President Kennedy told him in advance he would be needing funds for the space program. The president did not ask for money; instead he simply told him, "We are going to the moon and we want some money out of you." According to Stennis, he emphasized that regardless of the cost, the mission was essential for our times.[3]

Stennis was somewhat taken back by his direct approach, but he liked Kennedy and was certainly willing to help support the space program. The successful launching of Sputnik by the Russians in 1958 shook the nation. Now Russia had a rocket that could launch a nuclear warhead to America, though Stennis doubted they could deliver an accurately placed warhead. He believed the United States still maintained weapon superiority, but he worried we could lose this lead if the space and missile program were not better organized and financed.

While their views on civil rights differed, Stennis liked Kennedy and wanted to work with him. He often joked that Kennedy did not ask, but told him that he expected Stennis's support of the space program.
(Courtesy Kemper County Historical Association)

Stennis was wary of three services—Army, Navy, and Air Force—competing for favor and funds from Congress. He also recommended the missile program be investigated, "The advent of the Russian satellite at this point can prove a blessing to us, if it jars us into a more realistic approach to our own military program and planning."[4] He had expressed serious concerns in 1957 when the U. S. did not launch its Vanguard satellite as planned. He accepted the failure as progress, but objected to the public announcements which "caused people to lose faith entirely in our missile program."[5]

Stennis did believe that keeping information from the public was justifiable if it was in the best interest of the nation. In a meeting with President Kennedy on September 20, 1961, Kennedy mentioned plans for a new space program facility in Louisiana.[6] According to Stennis, "I went to work....I went to my friend Senator Bob Kerr of Oklahoma, who was chairman of the Senate Space Committee. I had studied the requirements rather well and knew this facility would have to be accessible to a large body of water... He agreed. Fortunately, there were no nearby oceans in Oklahoma."[7]

The Logtown community in Hancock County, Mississippi was selected as a test facility for static firing Saturn V rocket engines for the Apollo manned lunar landing program. As a result, almost three thousand local citizens had to give up land their families had farmed and logged for decades. Stennis visited the community and was instrumental in convincing them of the importance of the Mississippi Test Facility to the people of Mississippi and the nation.

Stennis, always a strong advocate for military superiority, believed that the country that controlled space controlled the earth.[8] Stennis heeded the "Mississippi Comes First" placard on his desk by locating the test facility in Mississippi rather than in any other state. He was serious about serving Mississippians and would even delay meeting the president to meet with his constituents. Former Mississippi Commissioner of Agriculture Lester Spell recalls meeting with Stennis on a local water project when a staff member interrupted, telling Stennis that the president wanted to talk to him. Stennis told the staffer that the president would have to wait because "He had Mississippi people in his office."[9]

The Kennedy administration quickly faced a world in crisis. The Soviet Union was making good its promise of Communist domination. With Cuba such a short distance from Florida, Stennis believed the United States could ill afford to have the enemy so close. "I wholly reject the idea of peaceful coexistence with Castro. We cannot coexist with evil. Nor can we rest easy with Communist tyranny and military might ninety miles from our shores. We must treat Castro like the international outlaw that he is."[10] Although Stennis supported the Bay of Pigs invasion, it was a complete disaster for Kennedy and the nation. The Cuban exiles supported by the CIA were quickly defeated by Castro forces.

Realizing that the two super powers must communicate, Kennedy sought a nuclear test ban treaty with the Russians. Stennis was reluctant to accept Russian promises, "I share with my fellow Americans the understandable desire for peace and a peaceful world but I am not yet convinced that peace lies in the direction which this treaty—admittedly a first step—leads. Thus my vote against ratification of the treaty was not a vote against peace; it was against degrading the military superiority which alone has allowed us to maintain the peace for two decades."[11] As chairman of the Preparedness Investigating Sub-Committee in the Armed Services Committee, Stennis did not want to sacrifice military might to a treaty the Russians were unlikely to honor.

Later Stennis visited the Soviet Union to meet the enemy face to face. In 1958 Stennis spent nineteen days in Russia, Czechoslovakia, Poland, and Yugoslavia. He saw and talked to all types of people and was appalled at signs stating "We Must Bury America." But he was impressed with the people. He found them to be "alert, active, industrious, eager to learn, and above all, willing to pay the price of advancement." He was most impressed by their advances in education, which required all students to master the more difficult courses. "I found the children to be neat, bright, and eager. They meet and master the hard subjects in their early years: algebra in the fifth grade, for example. All courses are hard. All courses are required. There are no electives."[12]

While he never recommended adopting anything based on Soviet methodology, he suggested that American students "haven't had enough of that fine building drilled into them that will make them able to meet situations that I think we're going to be confronted with. We put off the day that we're going to have to do the hard things."[13]

Stennis spent considerable time on his visit observing Russia's younger generation, to gauge the caliber of the people who would later be running the country. Instead of the downtrodden, depressed youth longing for freedom that he had imagined, he saw a vibrant young Russia.

Stennis believed that Russia represented our greatest enemy, but he did not think they would attack the United States as long as our military strength was maintained. On the December 6, 1959, TV program "Face the Nation" Stennis expressed doubts that we were producing enough Polaris missiles for defense, or quickly developing a booster for space shots. The next month the administration approved seventy more Atlas and Titan missiles. While he did not take credit for this increased production, Stennis certainly approved their actions.[14]

Stennis always fought for a strong military. He wanted citizens to ensure their freedom by controlling inflation; eliminating slow-downs in manufacturing; providing technical aid and training for those countries who might otherwise become enemies; and "tightening the education system," stating, "our youth must be led away from rather than into a soft life."[15] Stennis believed that people who enjoyed the freedoms allowed here should become educated and productive citizens. Stennis pushed himself to do as much work as possible; he expected others to do the same.

On July 20, 1961, Stennis, as chairman of the Senate Military Preparedness Sub-Committee, attended a luncheon in the White House with newly elected President John F. Kennedy and other leaders. An assessment of the Asian situation was given by retired General Douglas McArthur. The senator's concern about unilaterally sending troops to Asia was reinforced by McArthur, who said that the Chinese Communists could match them [U. S.

troops] one hundred to one.[16]

As with Korea, the old general's knowledge of that part of the world was dismissed.

The Kennedy administration would face challenges from the Soviet Union during the Berlin Crisis in September 1961, and during the Cuban Missile Crisis in August 1962—all the turmoil created by Russia. At one point, Stennis suggested the Kennedy administration break diplomatic ties with the U.S.S.R., accusing the administration of being "too timid" to use diplomatic and economic pressures on the communists.[17]

Not taking Stennis's advice, Kennedy continued to communicate with Khrushchev and probably averted a direct confrontation.

Stennis and his Preparedness Investigating Subcommittee looked into allegations that U. S. Army General Edwin Walker was using his position to indoctrinate soldiers under his command with anti-Communist statements and John Birch Society literature. Questioning his right to make anti-Communist statements about Moscow against the wishes of the State Department, Walker was relieved of duty. Stennis's committee looked into Walker's activities and those of others in the military who were speaking without permission from the Department of Defense. Stennis took this responsibility seriously. He consulted with former President Dwight Eisenhower as well as Admiral Arleigh Burke and General Thomas White. In a newsletter Stennis reported that "our hearings would be complete and exhaustive, with nothing held back. It has been and will continue to be my purpose to get at the real facts, letting the chips fall where they might and sparing no department and no single individual who might be involved. If there is even one person…seeking to destroy our way of life, that is one too many and if he has worked for only ten minutes, that is ten minutes too long."[18]

Stennis was recognized for his fair treatment of all of the witnesses. He refused to sensationalize the hearings, hoping to avoid full investigations of the Departments of State and Defense. As a result, all had a chance to speak, allowing the subject to "drag on to the final dreary session." Justifying the length of the hearings, Stennis commented, "The committee was an arm of the Senate, and I believe in the Senate."[19]

Stennis was often given investigative assignments in the Senate, because his fellow senators knew he would be fair. Above all, he would not embarrass the Senate as an institution. In this case he had prevented embarrassment of the Department of Defense. As a favor to Stennis for his "judicious" handling of the hearings, Secretary of Defense Robert McNamara agreed to speak at Millsaps College in Jackson, Mississippi on February 24, 1967.

In many situations, Stennis did not think that hearings, especially public hearings where security issues were discussed, were needed. He preferred for Senate sub-committees to investigate and suggest remedies without the pomp and circumstance of a hearing.

With the civil rights issue foremost of the minds of Mississippians, Stennis's support of Kennedy in the 1960 election became problematic. Calling the 1960 Democratic platform the most sweeping party platform in American History in its support of civil rights, Stennis suggested to Senator Russell that the administration could not expect their support on domestic issues. Ironically, Stennis was often criticized for not vehemently opposing the civil rights movement as did Mississippi Governor Ross Barnett.

At the same time, Stennis was attacked by voters in other states for doing too much to preserve segregation. Knowing that Bilbo had been refused his Senate seat earlier, an Ohio doctor believed that Stennis should be treated similarly. The doctor received a blunt rebuke from his senator, Steven Young. The first sentence of Young's reply set the tone, "Just why would I do a foolhardy, stupid thing like that?"[20] Young explained that Stennis was well respected in the Senate and if nominated for a Supreme Court seat, would receive unanimous confirmation by the Senate.

The doctor appreciated the explanation and commented, "It is reassuring to know that he is so well qualified a person. We need as many men of his caliber in the Senate as we can get."[21]

Stennis's views on segregation differed from that of northern senators, but they still respected him as a colleague and a person. One Massachusetts Senator wrote, "But the part that I like best, whether we agree or not, is that

I know you are sincere and objective in your position. We are friends and I look forward to working with you this year again."[22] He shared personal friendships with many of his colleagues from the North, often corresponding during the years after they left the Senate.

While Stennis was tending to national issues, he had to also consider what was going on in Mississippi politics. Even though Ross Barnett never made a formal statement of his intention to challenge him in the next election, Stennis and his staff strongly believed Barnett would oppose him in the 1964 election. In addition, Stennis saw his traditional Mississippi Democratic Party being attacked at their convention in Atlantic City by the Mississippi Freedom Democratic Party. Its members claimed they had been disenfranchised by the regular Democratic Party. For a time, a battle was fought over which group would be seated at the convention. When the compromise required the regular Democrats to sign a pledge supporting the party platform, they walked out in protest. At the same time, the Mississippi Freedom Democratic Party, led by civil rights activist Fannie Lou Hamer, vice-chair of the group, left very disappointed: they were only offered two seats.[23]

Many of the regular delegates preferred the Republican candidate, conservative Barry Goldwater.

Governor Ross Barnett became the state's flag bearer in opposing federal civil rights legislation. He urged Mississippians to resist the entrance of a black man, James Meredith, to the all-white bastion of Mississippi sovereignty, the University of Mississippi. An editorial in the *Meridian Star* labeled his stance ordering "state officials to enforce Mississippi segregation law regardless of orders of the U. S. Supreme Court" as "Barnett's Finest Hour"… "He deserves the support of every Mississippian during this terrible time of trial and crisis."[24]

Many of his supporters believed he could defeat John Stennis, who was considered weak by some for not advocating the use of any means to halt desegregation.

Stennis was among those labeled a "loyalist" for supporting John F.

Kennedy in the 1960 presidential election. Afterwards, Stennis wrote in a memo for his files that the race problem hung over Mississippi "like a dark cloud…if Mississippi could get out from under this burden, we would enter a new and higher plateau."[25]

Nonetheless, Stennis believed the 1960 election was good for the voters in the state; it made them more aware of the issues, especially racial issues, which were dividing the nation. In a meeting in 1963 with a Mississippi legislator, Joseph E. Wroten, Stennis applauded Wroten's stand on civil rights. Wroten was one of the two votes in the Mississippi House opposing Barnett's attempts to prevent James Meredith from entering the University of Mississippi in 1962. Stennis admitted to Wroten that in order to keep his office he could not express his true feelings. He justified this position by saying that he could do more for Mississippi if he remained in the Senate. Stennis urged Wroten to continue his efforts on behalf of civil rights. Branded a "scalawag" by some, Wroten was not able to influence the Mississippi House much longer; in 1964 he was defeated for his support of civil rights.[26]

Mike Espy, former U. S. Secretary of Agriculture and a U. S. Representative, considered Stennis to be a "statesman," but before he could become a "statesman," he had to be a politician. As a politician Stennis had to conform to the white electorate in order to become a "statesman."[27] Stennis could not show any reluctance to attack civil rights legislation, thereby giving Barnett ammunition to run against him.

Concerned that Mississippi's electoral votes were "unpledged" and did not go for John Kennedy in the 1960 election, Stennis wrote to friend and supporter William Winter that he had been "trimmed back to what personal influence he had….I am not complaining about this because instead of looking back, I always try to work with what tools I have."[28] Stennis considered himself a Southern Democrat, "but I am entirely a free agent to use my own judgment, without any obligation to follow a party line which I think is unsound. I strive to be an effective Senator."[29] Regardless of his partisan politics, Stennis did have a great deal of personal influence. He was well respected by other Senators, and his counsel was often sought.

Stennis was concerned that Barnett would challenge him. He joined Representatives Abernathy, Whitten, Winstead, Williams, and Colmer, and Senator Eastland, in sending a telegram to Barnett two weeks prior to the Ole Miss riot, "We congratulate you on your effort and determination to preserve the sovereign rights and privileges of our state and pledge you and the people of Mississippi our full and unqualified support."[30] Knowing Barnett's popularity, Stennis probably did not want to be singled out as one of Mississippi's delegation in Washington who did not applaud Barnett's stand. Stennis later moderated his full support of Barnett by stating that the situation "raises the grave and serious question of interposition, I certainly will study it with the greatest interest and concern."[31] Stennis often did not give a direct answer to a question or action, preferring this delaying tactic. If pressed and without time for study, he could refuse support. In this case time was running short. The Meredith issue was heading to a showdown. Few knew that Barnett and the Kennedy brothers were "making deals under the table."

Barnett and the Kennedy administration were communicating in an attempt to allow Meredith to enter Ole Miss and still have Barnett seen by the public as a hero. In one scenario, Barnett wanted to temporarily block Meredith's entrance, but would step aside when faced with federal officials who carried revolvers. This idea was rejected; guns would be displayed by federal officers.

Both President John Kennedy and Robert Kennedy underestimated Barnett's ability to manipulate them. Barnett never went on campus, and he neglected to provide the promised protection by the Mississippi Highway Safety Patrol for the federal marshals escorting Meredith. Barnett sent Lieutenant Governor Johnson instead, who could not act officially as long as Barnett was in the state. The resulting riot claimed two lives and numerous injuries to rioters and federal marshals. Ironically, the marshals would have been overrun had it not been for the Mississippi National Guard. The all-white guard unit at Oxford opposed Meredith's entrance, but once federalized, they obeyed presidential orders.[32] Militarily, the Ole Miss situation was unusual; the orders were given them directly from the White House.

As soon as Stennis learned of the crisis at the University of Mississippi, he requested that President Kennedy remove Meredith immediately from the campus to prevent additional violence. Meredith remained, but Stennis was successful in having black soldiers removed from the Ole Miss campus and halting the construction of a military facility to serve federal troops at the Oxford airport.

Most of the letters Stennis received on Meredith's entry into Ole Miss very forcefully stated that Meredith should be removed, and that the President should be impeached. A few letter writers had opposing views, "I am sure that the same thought occurs to you as it does for me when I see a Negro—there for the grace of God go I. It is hard enough, indeed, for persons with all of the advantages of our society to become a success and for an individual who is qualified in all other ways with the exception of his color to be denied the educational opportunities…certainly undemocratic," said one writer.[33] After requesting that Meredith be removed she added, "I think one of the greatest causes of our being lowest among the states in capital wealth is the fact that the Negro has not been allowed to develop himself to the greatest possible point."[34]

When later asked for an opinion of Stennis, Meredith simply said, "He was smarter," meaning that even though Stennis was not as vocally racist as were his Southern contemporaries, he wanted to maintain a segregated society.[35]

Both Governor Ross Barnett and Lieutenant Governor Paul Johnson were in contempt of court for their actions. But no charges were filed. The Kennedy brothers believed that additional coverage would only make them heroes, possibly giving Barnett additional confidence to challenge Stennis in the upcoming 1964 election.

Given Barnett's popularity, Stennis prepared for a state-wide campaign similar to his 1947 efforts to ensure victory.

The Senator's friend and confidant J.P. Coleman wrote in March 1963 that a Mississippi College professor proclaimed that Barnett could beat Stennis.[36] Confiding to Stennis staffer Marx Huff, Coleman was concerned that Stennis had not begun his campaign early enough to discourage opposition.

Knowing that the campaign would be expensive, Stennis asked his son, John Hampton, to find out what previous state-wide elections cost. John Hampton replied that one-quarter of a million dollars would be needed when facing a strong primary opponent and a possible independent in the general election. Having a large campaign fund would discourage others from running.[37] To raise that amount of money, Stennis returned to his tried and trusted county support system that had served him so well back in the 1947 election.

By January 1, 1963, Stennis wanted his campaign workers to be organized. A county committee headed by a chairman with a small sub-committee for making quick decisions would be instituted. Stennis wanted representation on the committee from every precinct with more than thirty to forty voters. He emphasized that each committee should have young people as well as women. The committee should include "blue collar" workers and "those from different walks of life" that "do not ordinarily get a chance to take part in public affairs." Precinct captains would be in charge. To solicit their support, but at the same time preserve their neutrality, he advised against asking county officials to be on the committees, but suggested they act as advisors.

His organizational instructions reflected his political acumen, "We have a 16-year record that is sound and conservative, and one which will meet the approval of a great majority of people. However, 'a good record' is not enough to win. To win an election these days, a man must have not only a good record but lots of working friends. We will fight clean, and we will fight hard. By all working together, we will win. But a lot of work will be required, and we must start early."[38]

In planning his campaign organization, Stennis wanted to know if Barnett would really challenge him.

Going back to his confidence in the courthouses for support, Stennis instructed his representatives in each county to ask their county leaders for support, and at the same time see if anyone else was making "soundings" about running for the U. S. Senate. He wanted his supporters to reiterate, "That I am a Senator of and for the people of Mississippi solely—and that I have no connections here that make me obligated in any other way; I am *not* pro-Kennedy and I am *not* for Kennedy; and that I have one of the most conservative voting records in the Senate."[39] Stennis wanted to distance himself from President Kennedy and his brother, Robert Kennedy, the Attorney General, who were, to say the least, extremely unpopular in Mississippi. They were blamed for the Ole Miss riot and the push for the desegregation of the South. Stennis liked President Kennedy, but he needed to distance himself from him at this time. Later, Stennis was shocked when he learned of Kennedy's tragic assassination, feeling that the country had lost a great leader.

Not all Mississippians had negative opinions of President Kennedy. Stennis received a letter from a seventy-five-year old Kemper County resident who wanted Stennis to accompany President Kennedy to their place for the celebration of the one hundredth birthday of a neighbor who had voted for President Kennedy. "We live in a humble house on the side of the road," she wrote. "It is hoped that your helicopter [will] jump down here."[40]

Stennis received a number of unusual requests from his constituents who believed he could fulfill them. While he might laugh in amazement at some, he was interested and always replied.

In addition to Barnett, Representative John Bell Williams was mentioned as a possible contender in the 1964 election.[41] With the popularity of Barry Goldwater in Mississippi, Wirt Yerger Jr., Mississippi Republican Party Chairman, believed that Charles L. Sullivan could defeat Stennis if he ran as a Republican. Yerger also believed that Democrat John Bell Williams, who publicly supported Goldwater, had a good chance of defeating Stennis.[42]

Knowing others could challenge him, Stennis wanted to be ready so that he "would not be subjected to harassments by small, special groups who might try to extract promises at the last. In other words, I want to have affirmative strength of my own already organized in order to meet any development—whether that development is real or threatened."[43]

In 1963 the Mississippi State University basketball team won the SEC title and the opportunity to play in the NCAA tournament in Michigan. The opponent's team would have black players. Mississippi State had withdrawn from the tournament the past two years for that reason. The SEC Commissioner expected State to do the same in 1963. However, MSU President Dean Colvard allowed them to compete after contacting Senator Stennis. His opinion counted. Stennis encouraged participation, but stated he could not make a public statement for fear Barnett would use the decision against him in the 1964 election.

Colvard understood Stennis's predicament, "I never held that against Stennis because that was reality. I had no doubt at all that Barnett would use whatever tool he could play and I did not want to see him beat John Stennis. John Stennis was the strongest supporter I had in Mississippi, and the last thing I wanted to do was sacrifice him for me."[44]

Colvard's decision was vigorously challenged by segregationists statewide including members of the College Board. Their proposal to prevent the trip was defeated. To show board support, Colvard received a nine to two confidence vote. S.R. Evans, one of the senator's staunchest supporters, served on that board. No doubt, he and Stennis had talked.

The team went to Michigan, but not before Colvard and basketball coach Babe McCarthy avoided an injunction by leaving the state the night before the game.

Finally, one of Stennis's county representatives wrangled a decision from Barnett on Christmas Day, 1963. Ray M. Sartor from Ripley was talking to Barnett by phone when Barnett told him he was not going to be a candidate in the upcoming senatorial election. When Sartor relayed the message to Stennis, who was at home in DeKalb, Stennis was skeptical. To remove any doubt, Stennis himself called Barnett, who confirmed he would not challenge him.[45]

One rumor circulated that Eastland had convinced Barnett not to challenge Stennis, but to run for Governor in 1967.[46]

Barnett, however, waited until February 12, 1964 to make a public announcement that he would not run. He was so involved in the governorship that he could not consider running for any other office, "Frankly, I have never considered becoming a candidate for the United States Senate."[47]

With the threat of Barnett behind them, Stennis learned he would have a black opponent in the Democratic primary. Victoria Gray was one of the black Freedom Democratic Party leaders who challenged the regular Democrats at the Atlantic City National Convention. Stennis did not worry about Gray's challenge. He turned his attention to foreign affairs.[48]

President Johnson and Vietnam

When Lyndon Johnson became president after John F. Kennedy's assassination, he pledged to follow Kennedy's plan to support efforts to keep South Vietnam free from Communist control. Without the knowledge of Congress, covert activities sponsored by the United States provoked the North Vietnamese into attacking a U. S. Navy ship, the *U.S.S. Maddox*, in the Gulf of Tonkin.[49] The Tonkin Gulf resolution was passed, giving the president the power to defend U. S. interests, using both air power and ground troops if needed without a congressionally approved, formal declaration of war.

While Stennis would later question the authority of the president to begin such a conflict, he now told the Senate, "We dare not run away, certainly while we are under attack."[50]

After Johnson's election in November 1964, bombings of North Vietnamese targets began. In March two Marine battalions were sent to provide protection at the air base in Danang. Stennis's comment was, "As always, when we send one group, we shall have to send another to protect the first, and we shall thus be fully committed in a short time."[51]

As a member of the Armed Services Committee, Stennis was concerned with the Defense Department's budget request for supplemental appropriations due to greater involvement in Vietnam. As chairman of the Military Preparedness Subcommittee, Stennis wanted the military to be well prepared and supplied. He often doubted Secretary of Defense Robert McNamara's programming, planning, and budgeting method of funding the various services, which often left military units with insufficient supplies.

In a July 1965 report, Stennis declared there were "serious deficiencies and inadequacies in Army readiness."[52] He believed that the increase in supplies and men in Vietnam jeopardized our defense capabilities in other parts of the world: "It should be more than obvious that the United States cannot alone protect the free world against the aggressive and expansionist designs of Communist nations indefinitely."[53]

At this time, Stennis steadfastly supported the president in the war effort. An October 1965 letter congratulated the president on his firm foreign policy stand which put more troops in Vietnam.[54] He was confident in the ability of the military. But as the war continued he became critical of the administration's failure to consult military leaders about bombing targets in Vietnam. The conflict was being run from the White House rather than the battlefield. Much like in Korea, the military was fighting with one hand tied behind its back.

In speeches and television commentaries, Stennis recommended that the military do what was necessary to win the war, even if the Chinese, who were backing the North Vietnamese, became engaged. Backing out without victory would only lead to other confrontations. He did not preclude the use of nuclear weapons if the lives of American soldiers could be spared.

These comments further stiffened the resolve of the growing anti-war movement. Stennis had little use for those in the anti-war movement in the U. S., but the anti-war movement in South Vietnam did capture his attention.[55]

When protesters in South Vietnam called for a U. S. exodus, Stennis questioned why American soldiers should be fighting for the independence of a people who did not want them involved. Stennis remained concerned about U. S. allies' lack of support. At the same time, he believed the administration was supplying insufficient information about the war. The senator's

*As fellow senators, Johnson and Stennis got along well. Initially, Stennis supported John-
son's war effort in Vietnam. Later, when Stennis believed that military decisions were being
made by the White House, he opposed Johnson's war policies. Stennis did not agree with
Johnson's plans for "A Great Society," as he thought it removed an individual's incentive to
work and be responsible for their own actions.
(Courtesy Kemper County Historical Association)*

Senate Preparedness Investigating Subcommittee pushed for more information in hearings held in August 1967. The hearings were closed to the public. Stennis chose to release the opening statements after military leaders testified. According to their testimony, the joint chiefs of staff were not invited to presidential planning meetings that designated bombing sites. Johnson and his secretary of defense, Robert McNamara, were approving the areas to be bombed. Not wanting to incite the Chinese and the Russians, they determined not to bomb populated areas or mine the harbors where the enemy was receiving supplies. Johnson believed a program of "gradualism," continual bombing, would force negotiations.

Stennis, on the other hand, wanted an all-out bombing effort to bring the enemy to the negotiating table. When McNamara testified before the subcommittee he defended the president's actions, reiterating that no all-out bombing campaign would force the enemy to withdraw from South Vietnam.[56] Stennis was worried that Vietnam was undermining military effectiveness in other areas since McNamara had instituted a military savings program. He questioned McNamara about the actual costs of the conflict. McNamara said he did not know the costs. Stennis replied, "Well, Mr. Secretary, if you do not know how much you're going to spend, how can you say how much you're going to save?"[57]

Stennis had reasons to be suspicious. He earlier spotted $300,000 of questionable expenses in a one billion dollar appropriation bill. He reported this to Deputy Secretary of Defense Cyrus Vance. "Cy, this … is a vivid illustration of how our government is running down hill with all the brakes off….I actually do not believe there were over two Senators that realized the implications … even in a small degree, and those two did not fully realize."[58]

As more and more troops were committed to the Vietnam conflict, Stennis warned, "The time has come for the administration to win the war instead of trying not to lose it."[59]

On the ground, U. S. commander General William C. Westmoreland requested more troops, but McNamara denied his request. Stennis agreed with Westmoreland. For his support of the war effort, he was deemed a war hawk by the growing number of Americans who opposed the conflict. Stennis was supportive of the troops, but in an appearance on CBS's "Face the Nation" on April 2, 1967, he criticized the Johnson administration's war policies.[60]

Later the next month, in a surprise move for everyone, including President Johnson, McNamara pushed for a negotiated settlement rather than a victory. After tendering this suggestion, he resigned his position as secretary of defense.

The anti-war supporters held a large rally in October 1967 in Washington, D.C. Stennis announced that the rally was partially sponsored by the American Communist Party in concert with the Viet Cong. Due to his deep patriotic beliefs and World War II memories, Stennis had no use for war protesters whose efforts might lower the morale of this country's fighting men.

The war escalated. The Viet Cong launched their Tet offensive January 31, 1968. Practically every city in South Vietnam, including the U. S. embassy in Saigon, was attacked. Although the attack was repulsed, the "restricted warfare formula" of the administration came into question. Stennis blamed the administration's failure to provide necessary military support and insisted that a new policy be adapted. He would no longer support sending more troops to a war that could not be won.[61]

Stennis and Johnson were old friends, so it was difficult for the Senator to criticize him openly. Stennis complained to Senator Richard Russell that "the war situation …looks mighty bad and is making my hair gray. The President is really under great strain."[62]

On March 31, 1968, Johnson announced a unilateral reduction in Vietnam forces.

He also shocked the nation by announcing that he would not seek another term. His decision was based on a number of factors: the public's sinking confidence in his Vietnam policies; an upcoming battle with Robert Kennedy to gain the Democratic nomination; and his health problems. According to his wife, Lady Bird, the betrayal of friends "destroyed us."[63]

While she had mentioned no names, Stennis could have been among those she felt had betrayed her husband. In an attempt to garner support for the Democratic Presidential nominee Hubert Humphrey, Johnson ordered a halt to all military actions in North Vietnam. But it was Republican Richard Nixon, vowing to end the Vietnam War, who won the election.

When Senator Russell became chairman of appropriations in 1969, Stennis assumed chairmanship of the Armed Services Committee. More opposition to the Vietnam War meant that military expenditures were questioned. Stennis, who been taught that waste was a sin, nevertheless fought to insure that the military had what was needed to defend the country, "You must have the best....I don't think anyone is going to jump on us as long as we keep in shape."[64]

Wanting to hear all viewpoints, Stennis allowed dissent within the committee, something that Russell had not permitted. Stennis reminded military witnesses appearing before the committee that Congress was still in charge of their appropriations. In his testimony, the Secretary of the Navy John Chafee mentioned that funds for a new carrier came from reprogrammed money.

Stennis replied, "We might have put the wrong 100 folks in the Senate, but they are here under the process and they are entitled to the right to vote. Yes, you know I am for the carrier... put the carrier the right way and I support it."[65]

Considered one of the "Lions of the Senate," Stennis seldom wielded the power he possessed. When he became Chairman of Armed Services he held onto his position in the Preparedness Sub-committee even though Stuart Symington was in line for that chairmanship. Symington, a Missouri Senator who was once secretary of the Air Force, was qualified, but Stennis considered him to be too critical of the military. Symington resented this action and considered it a "snub."[66]

While acquiescing to the Pentagon's requests, Stennis opposed spending on most domestic programs. A Ralph Nader report stated that he voted "against welfare [by voting] against Medicare, against the poverty program, against model cities, against child care and development, coupled with legal services for the poor, against manpower training increases, and against food stamp increases—all of which were legislative proposals that spoke directly to the economic, welfare, and medical needs of the people in Mississippi, 45 per cent of whom have incomes beneath the federally established poverty level."[67] Those Mississippians who were below the poverty level and black did not vote. Most white Mississippians were against what they considered giveaway programs for blacks who did not want to work for a living. Others, including the president of the United States, did not agree with Stennis and the white electorate he represented.

President Johnson And Civil Rights

When President Kennedy was assassinated on November 23, 1963, Vice President Lyndon B. Johnson promised to continue Kennedy's civil rights programs. President Johnson pushed the 1964 Civil Rights Act through as a memorial to the former president. Title II of this bill eliminated discrimination in establishments serving the public. When asked by President Johnson if he would support the bill, Stennis answered that "his people would not go along with it." Johnson then told Stennis the following story about his White House cooks,

> Well you know, John, the other day a sad thing happened. Helen Williams and her husband, Gene, who have been working for me for many years, drove my official car from Washington down to Texas, the Cadillac limousine of the vice-president of the United States. They drove through your state, and when they got hungry, they stopped at grocery stores on the edge of town in colored areas and bought Vienna sausage and beans and ate them with a plastic spoon. And when they had to go to the bathroom, they would pull off on a side road, and Helen Williams, an employee of the vice-president of the United States, would squat in the road to pee. And you know, John, that's just bad. That's wrong. And there ought to be something to change that. And it seems to me that if the people in Mississippi don't change it voluntarily, that it's just going to be necessary to change it by law.[68]

Stennis could say little in defense of Mississippi, because he knew what Johnson said was true. Southern Democrats were surprised at Johnson's support of civil rights. Since he was a Texan, most southerners believed he would help maintain a segregated South. That understanding had made the Kennedy-Johnson ticket more palatable. Many white southerners felt betrayed with the passage of Johnson's 1964 Civil Rights Act.

Still hoping that Mississippians would obey the new legislation, Stennis expressed positive comments about the Mississippi Economic Council's resolution to comply with the civil rights legislation rather than advocate lawlessness. One constituent hoped Stennis would be "retired" in the next election for this view. Stennis replied that he wanted to keep his job, "But I had rather be defeated for doing the things which I think I should do, than be defeated for having the lack of courage to do what I think I should do."[69] According to Stennis, "Your representative owes you not only his industry, but his judgment; and he betrays instead of serves you if he sacrifices it to your opinion."[70]

After passage of the 1964 Civil Rights bill, Stennis wrote to his mentor and friend Richard Russell, "Except for you and your fine leadership, a strong Civil Rights bill would have been passed…as early as 1948 and the years soon thereafter or certainly soon after the Supreme Court decision of 1954."[71]

While they could not stem the tide of civil rights, they delayed it, giving the South some time to adjust.

According to the Senate Majority Leader Mike Mansfield, losing the fight on civil rights earlier could have divided the Senate for years. Mansfield thanked Stennis for helping prevent that division.[72]

For Stennis the Senate was the right place to debate important legislation like civil rights. Southern senators had fought a good fight, but they lost and would accept the will of the majority. Stennis did not change his views on civil rights. As a former district attorney and judge, however, he respected the nation's laws. He had to work within the law to try to keep southern schools segregated. If the new legislation was not followed, federal funds to local school districts could be withheld.

In the freedom of choice plans, black students who chose white schools were often harassed and separated from the white students. As a result, by 1966 less than one percent of Mississippi's black students attended white schools. The Health, Education, and Welfare Department (HEW) implemented tougher standards that required school integration. Stennis argued in the Senate that HEW had changed its mind so often that frustrated school officials did not know what to do next.

Stennis opposed President Lyndon Johnson's Great Society. He believed this tenet fostered a reliance on government that overshadowed personal efforts. Stennis wrote:

> Some major portions of the so-called Poverty Program and Great Society have already set in motion a trend that is ruining our country. The reason for this is that some of these programs actually teach many people that there is no need to work. It teaches some people not to work. Such a course is suicidal, under both natural law and divine law. We are in effect giving away money and things to people who can work, but will not. This practice will ruin the individual and eventually our country. I exempt from my remarks, of course, those payments for earned social security benefits, earned retirement, worthy welfare cases and those physically or otherwise unable to work.[73]

Stennis's opposition to Johnson's programs impacted many Mississippi blacks.

With the mechanization of agriculture, blacks who remained in Mississippi had few opportunities for work. Those in the Mississippi Delta, who once barely existed as sharecroppers, now depended on government assistance for food, housing, and medical care. Stennis, along with fellow Senator Eastland, successfully closed down the Office of Economic Opportunity's Child Development Group of Mississippi (CDGM) by claiming Communist connections and mismanagement by the black leadership. In addition to providing medical care and food for children, CDGM established one of the earliest Head Start programs. In spite of its progress, attacks by segregationists caused the program to be revamped with biracial leaders as the Mississippi Action for Progress program, which continues to manage Mississippi's Head Start Program.[74] Some reporters correctly suggested that Stennis challenged the CDGM program in order to "mollify his segregationist critics."[75]

The assassination of Senator Robert Kennedy prompted Stennis to write Johnson about, "the lawlessness and violence that has been allowed to envelop the nation.... The whole society is being gradually infected with the idea that laws are only for those who obey them, and violence and intimidation are acceptable methods of accomplishing any purpose."[76] Maintaining his high sense of justice, Stennis suggested that the president issue a proclamation urging that laws be enforced and violators be prosecuted.

Later, Stennis would become a victim of the lawlessness he deplored.

CHAPTER V
NIXON, FORD, AND CARTER YEARS

Nixon Ends Vietnam War

As a ranking member of the Armed Services Committee, Stennis was frequently consulted by President Nixon on military matters. Briefing Stennis and other congressional leaders would legitimize some of his clandestine actions in Vietnam. Nixon approved of bombing Viet Cong sanctuaries in neighboring Cambodia, but he did not want the public to know about these things. Military records were falsified to insure secrecy. When the military movements became public, Nixon claimed he had approval from congressional leaders, especially John Stennis.[1]

Nixon and his staff may have informed Stennis about military objectives, but they often neglected to provide details. Later, when the full extent of the situation became public, Stennis defended his support by saying he was not given all of the facts, especially in one situation involving the keeping of duplicitous records.[2]

This incident led to the forced retirement of Air Force General John C. Lavelle. Rather than tell the nation that Nixon had sanctioned the bombings in Cambodia, the administration chose to let Lavelle be the scapegoat, claiming that he had violated the rules of engagement and acted on his own in ordering his pilots to attack surface-to-air missile sites in North Vietnam as a precautionary measure.

Lavelle maintained his innocence at Senate Armed Services committee hearings chaired by Stennis in 1972. Stennis conducted the hearings fairly, giving everyone an opportunity to testify, especially Lavelle. At the close of the hearings, which lasted over three and one-half months, Lavelle was not awarded the higher rank of lieutenant general upon retirement. Stennis did not know that Nixon and his staff allowed Lavelle to take the blame. In 2010 the family's request to restore Lavelle's rank and reputation failed in the Senate, even though President Obama and Secretary of Defense Robert Gates supported reinstatement.[3] Had Stennis been aware of Nixon's actions, the outcome of the hearings would probably have been different.

Knowing how far Nixon and his administration would go to cover up their actions would certainly have made Stennis and others question Nixon's denial of future allegations involving Watergate. Stennis supported Nixon's Vietnam policy, including the bombing of Cambodia, as he believed that all possible should be done to end the war. He did not approve of military commanders conducting their own war without civilian oversight. As Chairman of the Armed Services Committee, Stennis would have known more than most about what was happening in Vietnam had he been given all of the facts. While he had cautioned entering the conflict when the first military advisors were sent by President Eisenhower, he maintained his "win at any cost" attitude almost to the end.

On January 23, 1973, a cease-fire agreement ended the Vietnam War. After eighteen years, the United States military left Vietnam to the Communist regime they were unable to defeat. Stennis was not pleased, but civil rights, more than Vietnam, remained the prominent issue in the South.

Nixon Appeases The South

Republican Richard Nixon, a supporter of neighborhood schools, gained support by expressing sympathy for the southern situation in his presidential campaign throughout South. Yet upon election, Nixon faltered on his promises. He supported the moves of Health Education and Welfare and the Justice Department to speed desegregation in the South. Stennis appealed to Nixon to muzzle HEW officials who threatened to withhold

As Chairman of the Armed Services Committee, Stennis was courted by the Nixon camp. Stennis was often briefed on the war in Vietnam to justify Nixon's decisions while some of the details were not discussed in the meetings.
(Courtesy Kemper County Historical Association)

federal education funds if districts did not follow their guidelines. According to Stennis, "Their apparent sole consideration is total and immediate integration, even if the schools are totally destroyed in the process."[4]

On July 3, 1969, HEW and the Justice Department demanded full compliance with all aspects of the civil rights legislation. With only a couple of months before Southern schools were to begin, Stennis, in a very uncharacteristic move, used his power to stifle Washington's efforts. While both Stennis and Nixon denied a *quid pro quo*, Stennis let it be known that the short timetable for Mississippi schools to meet HEW deadlines would cause confusion and possible chaos in his state.[5] He would need to go to Mississippi to help keep peace. At the same time, Nixon's Anti Ballistic Missile Treaty was being debated. As chairman of the Armed Services Committee, Stennis was guiding the controversial legislation, which he supported, through his committee. Nixon knew that the treaty would be in jeopardy without Stennis. He had often praised Stennis for his help. "This is just a note to tell you how much I appreciated your vote on the Safeguard system yesterday. In view of the enormous pressures built up in the news media and other quarters against the program, it took great political courage to stand up and be counted as you did."[6]

Much to the dismay of those in the administration who had been continually frustrated by one delaying tactic after another, HEW officials were put off once again. Nixon postponed the HEW deadline to December 1969. In the meantime, the Fifth Circuit Court fixed the date for implementation of the plans that would force the school districts to end the dual system. Not wanting to fight a court order, Stennis challenged HEW on the difference between *de jure* and *de facto* segregation as a means to force the North to desegregate as well.

Students attended schools based on where school district lines were drawn. Since black and white neighborhoods were often geographically separate, there was little change in the racial balance. HEW insisted that racial balance had to be obtained in the South, which had historically excluded blacks from white schools. At the same time, northern neighborhoods did not have to meet the same requirements. The South would have to use bus-ing to meet HEW requirements; the North would not.

Stennis believed that when other sections of the country were forced to follow the same rules imposed on the South, the HEW regulations would be relaxed. HEW officials disagreed with his reasoning, but agreed that school segregation existed in northern cities. Stennis proposed a nation-wide freedom of choice plan which was compromised in House-Senate con-ference committees. Ironically, his position was strengthened by a prominent, liberal, northern senator.

Democratic Senator Abraham Ribicoff of Connecticut added an amendment with stronger language to Stennis's bill to make northern states comply. When the amendment was defeated, Ribicoff accused his northern neighbors of hypocrisy: "They advocate strong action against segregation in the South, but do not want to enact the same approach toward the prob-lem in their own states. The question is whether Northern senators have the guts to face their liberal white constituents who have fled to the suburbs for the sole purpose of avoiding having their sons and daughters go to school with blacks."[7]

School integration was being forced on the South. Stennis, along with most of the other southern senators, fought the legislation. Stennis believed the public school system would be ruined if blacks and whites were deseg-regated. Some leaders even believed that public schools should be closed, but Stennis did not take such a radical approach. In some areas of the state, white academies were quickly established, leaving few white students in the public school system.

Stennis and Watergate

What started as an attempt to implant listening devices and remove files from the Democratic Party's offices in the Watergate Hotel in Washington, D.C. on June 17, 1972, ultimately ended with the resignation of a president. While President Nixon may not have sanctioned the break-in for the purpose of bugging the Democrats, he was quickly made aware of the incident and unwisely proposed a cover-up.

The existence of recordings of meetings in the Oval Office of the White House, where the cover-up was discussed, created a problem. Nixon refused to release the tapes, claiming executive privilege. Instead, he proposed that Senator Stennis listen to the tapes to see if they contained incriminating evidence. Nixon knew that Stennis had immense respect in the Senate, and he hoped Stennis would exonerate his actions. The Watergate special prosecutor, Archibald Cox, wanted the tapes surrendered to his office. Nixon had Cox fired by Robert Bork, the third-ranking member of the Justice Department. The "Saturday Night Massacre" was the result of Attorney General Elliot Richards' resignation along with the firing of his top deputy, William Ruckelshaus, for refusing to dismiss Cox.

In 1987 Bork was nominated to the Supreme Court by President Ronald Reagan, a controversial nomination which was scrutinized by Senate democrats. Stennis considered the appointment "one of the more serious appointments that has been made, one of the more important decisions I will have to make."[8] Whether Stennis was influenced by Bork's Watergate action is not certain, but Stennis was among the fifty-eight senators who voted against his nomination to the Supreme Court.

On October 12, 1973, the U. S. Circuit Court of Appeals upheld Judge John Sirica's request for the tapes. With this action, Nixon's plan to have Stennis review the tapes would be moot. At any rate, the Mississippi Senator was still recuperating from gunshot wounds received while being robbed in front of his Washington, D.C. home January 30, 1973.

Under court orders, Nixon was forced to release the tapes to the Special Prosecutor assigned to the case. Some believed Nixon chose Stennis because Nixon knew that Stennis's stellar reputation could vindicate him. The scenario never developed. However, Stennis stated publicly he would report what he found, even if it were damaging to President Nixon.

At 4:30 AM on August 8, 1974, the phone at the Stennis home rang. It was the White House calling. A weary President Nixon told Stennis, "I have let you and Miss Coy down."[9] That night Nixon told the nation in a special TV broadcast that he would resign. Friends from their Senate days together, Stennis and Nixon understood each other, and they maintained contact after his resignation.[10]

Even with all of the problems surrounding Watergate, Stennis did not support radical changes in the intelligence community. The Watergate burglars had ties to the Central Intelligence Agency (CIA). Senator William Proxmire introduced legislation to give the agency more congressional oversight. Senator Stennis submitted his own bill defending the agency, telling the Senate, "Spying is spying. You have to make up your mind that you are going to have an intelligence agency and protect it as such, and shut your eyes some and take what is coming."[11]

Over the years the CIA had been implicated in a number of questionable acts, and with the current administration, the concern from Proxmire and others appeared to be justified. Stennis did not want to restrict the president, so he staunchly defended the agency. However, after Vietnam he was concerned with the president's constitutional powers; he believed the decision to commit the nation to war was too big for one man to make.

The War Powers Act

When Stennis entered the Senate in 1947, he believed that the United Nations (UN) could act as the world's policeman and maintain peace, but he soon conceded, "We were over optimistic. We were thrust front and center into the field of international affairs following World War II. We necessarily became a super power—the unquestioned leader of the free world."[12] Concerned that the president of the United States could commit troops to a foreign conflict without congressional approval, Stennis co-authored the Stennis-Jarvis bill (S. 2956) in April 1972. This legislation would limit the time a president could send troops without congressional authorization. This bill died in conference, but its final version (H.J. Res. 542) was written into law on November 7, 1973, over the veto of President Nixon. Known as the War Powers Act, it limits the time that the president can send troops overseas to sixty days without a declaration of war. Still recovering from his gunshot wound, Stennis could not be present for the final vote, but he sent the following message, "It is of the utmost importance to the future of this nation that we not again slip gradually into a war that does not have the moral support and sanction of the American people."[13] Stennis may be remembered nationally as the leading hawk supporting the military in Vietnam, but most Mississippians remember his informed judgment and the things he did to improve their state.

President Gerald R. Ford Pardons Nixon

Soon after taking office, Ford pardoned Nixon in the Watergate burglary of 1974. After receiving mail questioning Ford's action, Stennis replied he was surprised, but had not been consulted. He would have preferred the judicial process had been completed, but in support of Ford's action stated, "The matter of a pardon is invested solely in the President."[14]

Stennis wanted to put Watergate behind the Nation in an effort to address future challenges. President Ford tried to reign in federal spending and he thanked Stennis for his vote to sustain a veto on a public works employment bill. Ford believed, "The best and most effective way to create new jobs is to pursue balanced economic policies that encourage the growth of the private sector without risking a new round of inflation. This is the core of my economic policy."[15] Seeing that Stennis also opposed excessive spending, Ford sent Stennis what was obviously a recruiting letter, "What America needs is a Republican Congress working for Republican goals. Unless more Republicans are elected in 1976, inflation and excessive deficit spending will continue....Without your help, we cannot elect more Republicans to Congress."[16]

If Ford was attempting to get Stennis to change parties, he was not successful. Stennis remained a Democrat even though his domestic policies were often closer aligned to those of the Republicans.

Upon learning of Ford's pardoning of Nixon, Stennis commented that he
was not consulted, but he believed that was within Ford's power and that
the nation could now "look ahead."
L to R: Stennis, Senator John Sparkman (AL),
Jennings Randolph (WV), and President Ford.
(Courtesy Kemper County Historical Association)

Stennis was a committed Democrat although his votes were based on how pending legislation would impact Mississippi. "I believe the nation is best served when we have two strong major political parties of about equal strength in the Congress, with some conservatives in each party. I am a Southern Democrat, but I am a free agent to use my own judgment, without any obligation to follow a party line which I think is unsound. I strive here to make an effective Senator."[17]

At the time Stennis was in office, the committee system superseded the party system. In committee, both parties would debate the issues and compromise on what they could support. Stennis liked to know how the vote would go before speeches were made on the floor. Following the rift in the Democratic Party over civil rights, Stennis and other Southern Democrats are credited with a political transformation which elevated the popularity of the Republican Party in the South.[18]

When the *SS Mayaguez* was stopped by the Cambodian Navy in international waters near Poulo Wai Island, President Ford took immediate military action. Fearing the crew would be taken to nearby Kho-Tang, Ford dispatched planes and ships to the areas. A Marine assault on Kho-Tang demonstrated to the Cambodians that even though the United States had abandoned Vietnam, they would defend their rights in international waters. The crew was returned, but fifty-one Marines were killed in the action. Ford defended his response to Congress, stressing his full compliance with the War Powers Resolution initially proposed by Stennis during the Nixon administration.[19] Stennis did not object to this decisive action by Ford to defend the nation, but he did not want the President's actions to lead to another Vietnam without the approval of Congress.

President Carter Targets the Tennessee-Tombigbee Waterway

Although the 234-mile Tennessee-Tombigbee Waterway was first suggested in the nineteenth Century, planning was not authorized by Congress until 1946 through legislation sponsored by Mississippi Representative John

E. Rankin. This project was controversial, to say the least. Even the secretary of the Army objected to Stennis's 1955 bill to provide the project more than twenty million dollars. Initial funds for on-the-ground projects were finally approved in 1964 for flood control improvements on the Tombigbee and all of its tributaries north of the Warrior River in Alabama. Stennis considered this expenditure, "really a sound investment in the future." Congressman Thomas G. Abernathy was credited with sponsoring the $400,000 appropriation in the House. Corps of Engineers Major General Jackson Graham testified on the 1 to 1.6 cost-benefit of the flood control project. The Corps estimated an eventual cost of $27 million.[20] Funds were appropriated in 1967 as the demand from Europe for Kentucky and Tennessee coal increased. Having a shorter route to the Gulf would benefit industries in these producing states and also provide a corridor for new industries in Mississippi and Alabama. President Richard Nixon signed the initial appropriation for construction and attended the first ground breaking at Columbus.[21]

Many did not share Stennis's enthusiasm for the waterway.

The project was opposed by the Environmental Defense Fund with backing from the Louisville and Nashville Railway Company and the Association of American Railroads. According to the National Taxpayers Union, "The country simply does not need to build an alternative to the Mississippi River. As we know only too well, the government's capital resources are limited….The Tenn-Tom is a terribly costly project which is based largely on potential, not existing traffic which will never materialize."[22]

To demonstrate the size of the project, they claimed that the amount of dirt moved to construct the waterway could build a 25 foot wall that was 20 feet wide stretching across the United States. The Corps of Engineers' initial environmental impact statement showed no significant environmental damage was anticipated, but the waterway width change from one hundred seventy feet to three hundred feet raised new concerns.

At times the project appeared doomed as litigations continued. Opposition in the Senate was strong with Senator Thomas Eagleton calling the project a "gigantic hunk of useless concrete."[23]

President Jimmy Carter singled out the project as a waste and sought to have funding cut. In 1977 Carter calculated that about $5 billion could be saved by eliminating eighteen water projects, including the Tennessee-Tombigbee. In addition to the project in Mississippi, Carter wanted to cut projects in House Majority Leader Jim Wright's district, as well as those in Senator Russell Long's state. Long was serving as chairman of the Senate Finance Committee.[24]

To show support for the Waterway, Stennis requested a hearing at Columbus, Mississippi in 1977, prior to his scheduled Senate Subcommittee on Appropriations hearing. Over 3,000 people attended in support of continuing the project. At the Washington hearing, congressmen and governors outnumbered other witnesses. Both Mississippi and Alabama pledged funds. Stennis suggested that Carter would realize the importance of the project once he knew the facts.

Stennis and others argued it would now cost more to stop construction and restore the area than it would to complete the waterway. Funding votes for the Waterway in Congress were close: 48 to 46 in the Senate and 208 to 198 in the House for the fiscal year 1982 budget. According to Columbus attorney Hunter Gholson, who represented the Tennessee-Tombigbee Waterway Development Authority, "the only thing that saved the Tenn-Tom appropriations on at least two occasions that I remember, was just the respect that the other senators had for Stennis. Nobody in the [19]80's at least the late [19]70's, early [19]80's, wanted to confront John Stennis on any head to head basis."[25]

Senator Stennis wanted to help Mississippians who had supported him in previous elections—giving them construction jobs, improving economic growth prospects, and providing back-up shipping to the Gulf. According to his son John Hampton, completion of the Waterway was one of his proudest accomplishments.[26]

While Stennis claimed that economics caused Carter to change his mind, Carter realized that with Stennis chairing the Senate Appropriations

Carter wanted to cut some of the water projects, especially the Tennessee-Tombigbee Waterway. With Stennis as chairman of the Senate Appropriations and Mississippi Representative Jamie Whitten chairman of the House Appropriations Committee, the Waterway construction continued. Carter claimed that history would decide if the waterway was worthwhile. Stennis believed that Carter was "too good of a man to be president." (Courtesy Kemper County Historical Association)

Committee, Eastland chairing Judiciary, and Representative Jamie Whitten in charge of Appropriations in the House of Representatives, the Waterway would be completed.

Vice President Mondale jokingly told a joint session of Congress that Stennis and Eastland "were humble men and fair-minded men, that they always believed everything should be [split] down the middle, 50-50, fifty percent for Mississippi and fifty percent for the rest of the nation."[27]

In spite of their differences over the Tenn-Tom, Stennis had considerable respect for President Carter. He once commented that he was too good of an individual to be president.[28]

Stennis's support of the Tenn-Tom along with other Mississippi water projects led Senator Mark Hatfield (R. Oregon) to conclude that "Mississippi, after 100 years of waiting, has finally found a way to get revenge for Reconstruction."[29] For his support, the John C. Stennis Lock and Dam near Columbus was named in his honor.

While not as controversial as the Waterway, Stennis wanted to add twenty-six Mississippi counties to the Appalachian Regional Program in 1967 when the program was renewed. The Senate Public Works committee did not want any Mississippi counties included, but Stennis was able to persuade them to include eighteen counties. In conference with the House and with the support of Mississippi's representatives, twenty counties were finally accepted.

Stennis was fond of standing outside his office in DeKalb and with outstretched hands pointing to the small surrounding hills, calling them the "Foothills of the Appalachians."[30] One-half of the Appalachian funds were used for highway construction and improvement projects.

In addition to being chairman of the Senate Appropriations Committee, Stennis was chairman of the Public Works Subcommittee and a member of the Agriculture and Related Agencies Subcommittee, Defense Subcommittee, HUD, and Transportation and Related Agencies Subcommittee. As a member of these committees, Stennis was also well positioned to make certain that the Natchez Trace was completed.

Completion of The Natchez Trace

The Natchez Trace served first as a Native American trail and later it became the return route by traders rafting their goods down the Mississippi and traveling by foot to their northern homes. In 1938 Congress authorized construction of the Natchez Trace Parkway, which would connect Nashville, Tennessee with Natchez, Mississippi. As with most federal projects, authorization and funding were not in sync. Less than one month after arriving in the Senate, John Stennis informed the Natchez Trace Parkway Association that he would "actively support every measure in Congress needed to further support this great work."[31] When the Interior Department considered dropping their parkway projects, Stennis used his influence to secure another source of funding. The Interior Department had considered turning the Natchez Trace construction over to the states through which it passed. As a member of Senate Public Works, Stennis secured $3 million for the Trace to be added to the new Federal Highway Act. Stennis wrote to an interested constituent, "I see no reason why we should not see the work continued on approximately this scale from year to year in the future until it is completed."[32]

Stennis justified finishing the Trace after traveling on the completed portion by considering three virtues, "First, in the preservation of areas of historic significance; second… in filling a useful and practical purpose of expanding our highway system; and third, as a means of recreation…and that it could be a defense asset should the need develop."[33] Concerned that the administration might fail to uphold the completion of the Trace by impounding appropriated funds, Stennis appealed and received support from the White House in 1974.

As the votes to fund completion of the Trace became closer Stennis called upon others to help.

Representative Jamie L. Whitten, as a ranking member of the House Appropriations Committee, fully supported the project, but was having trouble justifying the large expenditure in the face of demands to finish the interstate highway system. The Trace was competing with seven other park-ways for completion. Whitten viewed the project as going at a "snail's pace." He claimed some problems resulted from the failure to procure "promised right-of-ways." At the same time, he was pushing the House Public Works Committee to fund the Yellow Creek Port and the Tennessee-Tombigbee Waterway, so he was reluctant to ask for too much more. He wrote to Sten-nis, "We need to work things out where we can get 'the mostest for the least-est.'"[34]

Tired of lack of support from the Interior Department, Stennis in-formed the newly appointed Secretary of the Interior, Cecil D. Andrus, that he would like to discuss completion of the Trace with him prior to his ap-pearance before the Senate Public Works Appropriations sub-committee. The Secretary would certainly pay attention. Stennis was chairman of that committee.[35] Stennis's cohort in the Senate, Thad Cochran, claimed, "It took the Romans less time to build the Appian Way." He, along with other officials from Alabama and Tennessee were pushing for enough funding to complete the project.

The 444-mile parkway was finally completed in 2005, having taken the longest time for completion than any other parkway. Mississippians could now remove their "Complete the Natchez Trace" bumper stickers.

CHAPTER VI
THE ELECTION OF 1982

Other than his initial campaign in 1947 and the possible challenge by Governor Ross Barnett in 1964, Stennis had faced little opposition for his Senate seat. In some of the elections, his staff could not recall the names of those running against him. However, in the 1982 election his age, rather than his accomplishments, encouraged a formidable young Republican challenger, Haley Barbour.

In running against an incumbent senator, Barbour was battling history. Only two incumbent senators had been defeated since 1918 when U.S. Senators were first elected by popular vote. Byran "Pat" Harrison defeated Senator James K. Vardaman in the 1918 campaign and Theodore Bilbo defeated Senator Hubert D. Stephens in 1934. Due to Stennis's accomplishments and popularity, Barbour was careful only to infer that the senator's age limited his mental and physical stamina in serving the people of Mississippi for six more years.

The 81-year-old Stennis, on the other hand, felt he was physically and mentally capable of serving another term.

Several newspaper editors, including Wayne Wedie with the *Ocean Springs Record*, John Emmerich of the *Greenwood Commonwealth*, and Danny Richardson with the *Natchez Democrat,* voiced concern over Stennis's age, suggesting that he should step aside and let someone younger replace him.[1] Some family members as well as some of his friends in the Senate wanted him to retire, but he felt an obligation to those who had supported him though the years to continue. He commented, "I thought all along I would run again. I weighed the situation and with all the problems, couldn't find a place to stop. I thought I could be of some help and didn't feel like running away."[2]

Very few differences existed in the political philosophies of Stennis and Barbour, leaving age as the major issue. Barbour hoped to capitalize on the resurgence of the two-party system in Mississippi, and the popularity of President Ronald Reagan, a Republican.

Realizing his vulnerability on the age issue and fearing an upset, Stennis knew he would have to call on his supporters probably for the last time.

Stennis wanted to run the campaign as he did the in 1947 race, using volunteers and county organizations to help him get reelected. His supporters, on the other hand, begged him to hire a campaign manager to run a modern campaign. In the end both styles were used. They chose Raymond Strother as the professional manager. He was recommended after handling Russell Long's successful campaign in Louisiana. Stennis chose retired U. S. Marine Commandant Louis Wilson as his 1982 campaign chief. Stennis reported that Wilson, a 38-year veteran of the Marine Corps and a World War II Medal of Honor recipient, would run the campaign while he himself was taking care of senatorial duties in Washington. Stennis also picked Mississippi Representative Joe Blount, a 34-year-old attorney from Decatur, to be his campaign manager. Paul Lacoste, a Jackson businessman and civic leader, agreed to serve as his treasurer and finance chairman. However, Stennis left no doubt that he was in charge.[3]

In the initial meeting with the new campaign manager, Strother began to tell Stennis that he would have to change his campaign approach and do uncomfortable things in order to win. After Strother's presentation, Stennis got up from his seat, approached the consultant, put his arm around his shoulder and said, "We don't have to win."

In spite of his comment, Stennis did want to win, but he would not change his ways nor do anything deceitful to gain victory. Rex Buffington, Stennis's press secretary, remembered Strother declaring that Stennis's comment marked the lowest point in his campaign managing career.[4] Stennis finally agreed to use both, the old methods that were successful in the 1947 election and a modern publicity campaign managed by Strother.

Stennis began his campaign by squeezing visits into towns over the state to address civic clubs, renew acquaintances in the courthouses, and meet supporters between trips to Washington to handle Senate activities. Stennis would try to visit a half-dozen towns each day. With that schedule, night meetings were avoided when Stennis tended to ramble and reminisce.[5]

The League of Women Voters agreed to host a debate between Barbour and Stennis. Stennis wanted to participate; however, his supporters talked him out of it. Stennis was able to hold his own in a one-on-one discussion or when addressing a large group, but they were afraid he might make a mis-statement in a debate.

Although Stennis refused to debate, both candidates appeared together at the Mississippi Press Association in June. The extra seventeen minutes of rambling that Stennis tacked onto his allotted ten minutes caused some consternation in the audience. The appearance was not a debate, but Barbour felt Stennis faltered on some of the questions.

Since Stennis would not agree to a debate, Barbour supporters filmed the senator's annual "Hour of Accountability" press conference. They wanted to take clips from the Stennis presentation and insert Barbour's answers in a pseudo debate format. This innovative approach was foiled when the senator's long answers could not be packaged into sixty-second TV spots. According to Barbour, editing Stennis to allow enough time for a response would not have been fair to Stennis.[6]

When asked about a debate, Stennis replied that his record of thirty-five years was well known to the voters, and a debate would only give exposure to his opponent.

With his health problems of the past few years, some wondered if Stennis could maintain a vigorous campaign schedule. However, he had battled back from being shot in 1973, and showed no signs of being unable to carry on for another six years. He believed given his power and influence in the Senate, he owed it to the people of Mississippi to run again.[7] Although he had been in and out of the hospital prior to the election, Stennis remained healthy during the campaign. After the election, he commented that he only took two aspirins during the whole time.[8]

Barbour used partisanship by tying Stennis to liberal Democratic senators Ted Kennedy and Tip O'Neal, while extoling the gains made by his fellow Republicans, Senator Thad Cochran and Representative Trent Lott. As the executive director of the Mississippi Republican Party, Barbour had helped elect Senator Thad Cochran and had worked on the presidential races of Gerald Ford, John Connally and Ronald Reagan. He boasted of the inroads made by the Republican Party and their need to regain control of the U. S. Senate. In a survey Barbour mailed to voters in the state, he asked for opinions on the policies of Reagan and Kennedy, but did not even mention Senator Stennis. His failure to discuss issues affecting Mississippi in the survey was questioned by some local newspaper editors.

The Barbour campaign was stung when the Stennis camp used a video clip indicating endorsement from Republican Senator Barry Goldwater. Barbour had been confident that Goldwater would support him, but Goldwater's friendship with Stennis may have diminished his support. In addition, there was speculation that President Reagan had promised Stennis that he would not campaign for Barbour. Reagan did sign a letter seeking contributions for Barbour's campaign, but the thought was planted that even Republicans would like to see Stennis remain in the U. S. Senate.

In response to Barbour's claim that Republicans were now in control, Stennis told the groups he addressed that President Reagan called him for advice because of his experience.[9] Reagan also appreciated the Senator's voting for seventy percent of his proposals in 1981.[10]

To make matters worse for Barbour, a poll conducted by Mississippi State University had Stennis in the lead. Barbour's supporters claimed the poll was biased in favor of Mississippi State's most famous alumnus.[11]

Another poll by Peter Hart, Stennis's own pollster, taken in early fall, showed Stennis with sixty-one percent and Barbour with twenty-three percent, and the remainder undecided or not responding.[12]

Prior to the election, Stennis had received many invitations to speak to

Stennis was well respected by Reagan. In the 1982 campaign, Stennis's challenger, Republican Haley Barber, failed to get presidential support in Mississippi, leading some to claim that Reagan wanted Stennis, who supported many of his policies, to remain in office. (Courtesy Kemper County Historical Association)

various civic groups and associations throughout Mississippi. Stennis excused himself from many of them by saying he was busy in Washington taking care of the state's business. Noting that Stennis was not in Mississippi campaigning, Barbour insisted that Stennis was not physically able to campaign. When the Senate session ended, Stennis hurried back to Mississippi, determined to show the opposition he was up to the challenge. To prove his stamina, during the week of October 18th he campaigned in Jackson, Meridian, Kosciusko, New Albany, Tupelo, Okolona, West Point, Macon, Quitman, Waynesboro, Laurel, Hattiesburg, and Collins. Stennis spoke in eighty-one of Mississippi's eighty-two counties, but did not appear in Barbour's home, Yazoo County.

When Stennis spoke at the state's major political event, the Neshoba County Fair, August 5, 1982, a large banner in Stennis's campaign colors, red and blue, appeared near the speaker's platform reading: "Happy 81st Birthday Senator Stennis." Stennis was born August 3, 1901. Rex Buffington, Stennis's press secretary, was disappointed that the Barbour campaign, who denied responsibility for the sign, brought the age issue to the voter's attention when they had agreed not to mention age.[13]

Stennis's reply to the age issue was that being a senator was not a boy's job.[14]

Barbour countered that he was only a year younger than Mississippi Senator James Eastland when he won his first Senate seat in 1942.

After several references were made by Stennis in speeches about Barbour's age, Barbour again reiterated the need for a debate, so that the public could judge whether or not he was too young for the job. At the Neshoba County Fair, Barbour was critical of Mississippi's economic performance. Stennis gave the audience an opposite view, "I believe that we are standing on the threshold of a great era of growth. That's what made America—growth. We're already on the move."

Stennis was an optimist who saw possibilities in challenges. He characterized himself as the "battling lawyer" from Mississippi who would "not desert them [Mississippians] under any circumstances."[15]

Mississippi Governor William Winter, who followed Stennis's appearance at the fair, praised Stennis for his efforts on behalf of the state while predicting a bright future as well.

Stennis, known for his work ethic, would often repeat that "My work is my play." He appeared to enjoy the campaign.[16] While Stennis predicted the election verdict would be "no change" in the Senate, his supporters were concerned that Barbour supporters might attempt to catch Stennis in a political *faux pas*.

Joe Blount cautioned Stennis to be careful when television cameras were around. He was afraid the opposition might show Stennis faltering in a discussion, getting off the subject, or somehow revealing that he was not physically or mentally able to continue.[17] Longtime Stennis supporter J.P. Coleman warned Stennis in a letter that he heard of a plan to have Barbour supporters ask Stennis confusing questions after his speeches that could embarrass and provoke a "scene." Coleman warned Stennis that the election was "his to lose." He should not work "too hard" and lose the election on "some freak occurrence."[18] Coleman's concern was valid. Campaign manager Joe Blount said Barbour's people had a camera person filming Senator Stennis to catch him faltering to show that he was too old to be returned to Washington.[19]

To protect the senator's image and guard against accidental perceptions of his inabilities to serve another term, TV spots showed him looking over the areas he had helped, such as the shipyards in Pascagoula, without his comments.

Satirically, after the election *Esquire* magazine awarded him the "best non-speaking part in a political campaign."[20]

Those managing his campaign were concerned when an ABC crew filmed Stennis sitting between two farmers at the Copiah County Fair while pigs squealed in the background. They were afraid that the active pigs could be associated with Stennis's success in obtaining "pork barrel" legislation. However, most Mississippians were not too concerned about "pork barrel" legislation, especially when their state was the beneficiary.

Trying to show that Stennis missed many votes in the Senate, Barbour attacked his voting record. Stennis politely wrote Barbour sending him his record, which showed that except for his absence after the 1973 gunshot, he had an eighty-nine percent participation record for his thirty-five years in the Senate. The last two years, he had made over ninety-one per cent of roll call votes.

Stennis was forced to respond to rumors that once elected he would leave office, allowing Governor Winter to appoint himself to the Senate. Stennis answered the rumor, "Not a bit of a chance in the world....Facts change, of course. Now, there is no purpose like that. A man that spent 50 years in public life, he does not go out there and lie to the people. It's unthinkable."[21]

Mississippians realized that Stennis's seniority and his proven record of integrity were more important than his age. Combining his tried and proven 1947 election tactics along with modern televised campaign techniques, he was able to meet voters' expectations. Stennis was favored to win. In a segment on NBC news in September 1982, reporter Kinley Jones predicted the election's outcome, "Barbour is counting on cross-over votes from Democrats who agree with him that Stennis is too old to be reelected. But Stennis is a legend in this State. For many here, voting against him would be like trying to float up the Mississippi—impossible."[22]

Stennis won the November election with sixty-five percent of the vote, carrying all but two counties—Barbour's home county, Yazoo, and Rankin.

Considering the senator's previous stands on segregation, Barbour expected to win a high percentage of the black vote. The campaigns of Democrats Robert Clark and Wayne Dowdy for seats in the House of Representatives, however, had more influence than Barbour had anticipated. Both candidates supported Stennis and asked their supporters to vote for him. Their requests helped Stennis earn more of the black votes.[23]

Stennis's vote in the Senate to extend the 1965 Voting Rights Act influenced black voters as well.

Despite serving as one of the team captains for the opposition to the original Act, Stennis had voted for its extension. He needed the black vote, and his views on the race issue had also changed.[24] Many disagreed with his decision. His office received letters expressing disbelief that he supported extension of the Voting Rights Act.

Barbour, on the other hand, as chairman of the Mississippi Republican Party and chairman of the Mississippi Republican Party Election Law Task Force, had testified before the Subcommittee on Civil and Constitutional Rights House Committee of the Judiciary in Montgomery, Alabama on June 12, 1981. His testimony opposed extension of the Voting Rights Act.[25] Stennis did not mention Barbour's testimony in the election, but it is possible that the black community was, in fact, aware of Barbour's opposition to extending the act and his belief that it should apply to all states.[26]

The election was expensive. Barbour reportedly spent $1,108,835. Stennis spent $921,710. Stennis had launched the campaign with $37,521 in his treasury.[27] In earlier elections Stennis had not accepted contributions from out of state, but for this election he welcomed money from all areas. Political Action Committees (PAC) made major contributions to both candidates. Contributions from PACs representing, labor, defense contractors, petroleum refiners, homebuilders, and the National Rifle Association went to Stennis. Both national parties helped fund their respective candidates. Some of the PACs giving to Barbour included the Associated General Contractors, the Capitol Foundation, and Adolph Coors. To be safe some groups contributed to both candidates.[28]

After having been forced to spend much more money in the election than he thought necessary, Stennis supported campaign finance reform. His comment was, "[Y]ou know, in a poor state like Mississippi, it's just horrible that you have to raise, that a person like me, who had been in the Senate since 1947, would have to raise almost a million dollars to keep a seat against a young fellow who has never run for anything before."[29]

While Stennis regretted spending so much money, he held no animosity toward his opponent. Soon after the election, Barbour's law partner and cousin, William Barbour, was nominated by Senator Thad Cochran for a federal district judgeship. Stennis testified before the Senate Judiciary Committee on his behalf. Haley Barbour held Stennis in high regard. He had never said that Stennis was too old to be effective; he reminded voters that Stennis would need to serve for six more years.[30]

Haley Barbour admitted that had Stennis been 61 instead of 81 he would have voted for him himself.[31]

After the election Barbour spoke of changes he would have made in the campaign, but doubted they would have made any difference in the outcome. He was proud that the election was run on a "high plane" without the personal attacks prevalent in many campaigns. Polls taken after the election suggested that Barbour should run again.[32] Statewide exposure certainly gave him name recognition when he successfully ran for the Mississippi governorship in 2003. The voters returned him to that office in 2007.

After the election, Stennis appeared reenergized, ready to move ahead. "So instead of believing that we are headed downhill, I believe there is a lot coming up hill too, a lot of strength developing and a lot of solid things that will make our society even greater. So let's look up hill and develop and use the talent we have and improve it and work for the good of all. I really did get a lot out of that campaign…I'm a better Senator than I was before."[33] If his staff thought that Stennis would relax after the election, they were disabused of that notion. Instead of resting on victory, he instructed his staff to develop a comprehensive plan to address all upcoming issues that would impact Mississippi in 1983. For example, he wanted his staff to find out why the Farmers Home Administration would not lend money for home building in Mississippi. The interest rates were high, but he said that if they could pay the interest they should get the loan.[34]

He was especially interested in getting the Tombigbee project completed and earning revenue.

The recent election was the first real political challenge he faced since 1947. Stennis had moved among his constituents more and he really liked meeting people. Stennis could always remember names. Former Democratic Party Chairman and Stennis staff member Ed Cole was surprised at his astute recollection,

I was constantly amazed how he remembered the small things people did for him—seven, eight, nine races before. He would often have you drive up a back road to see some farmer who nobody knew about, and nobody knew Senator Stennis knew anything about. He never forgot them. There was never any misunderstanding about his upbringing and about his perception of classes. But he always said, "Yes Ma'am" to women. And he always treated people with a personal level of dignity. And everybody who had an encounter with Stennis generally left with a good feeling about it, and you know, whether he was black, no matter. But people generally had a good feeling about it. He was very easy to talk to, [he] paid attention. And I think what I have learned about all of this is that once you reach a certain level in status and intelligence, people begin to accept the inevitability of change and they don't resist it.[35]

CHAPTER VII
JOHN STENNIS, THE MAN

Respect

In his early Senate years, Stennis visited the Library of Congress every night for several months, learning the rules and how to be a good senator. For his efforts and abilities, he was quickly recognized by his colleagues.[1] The respect Stennis had from the other senators was something that most Mississippians never knew. When he was shot in 1973, the entire Senate was stunned and shocked, knowing that his leadership and wisdom would be missed should the wounds prove fatal. He returned months later to a standing ovation and welcoming speeches by over one-half of the Senate.

A high school girl in Mississippi wrote Massachusetts Senator Edward Brooke, an African American, and asked what he thought of Senator Stennis. Brooke said, "Few votes are changed by debates on the floor except in John Stennis's case. When he talks, we listen, and he has been known to change votes, including mine."[2]

Unlike fellow Senator and President Lyndon Johnson, Stennis never told any other member how to vote on an issue. Stennis sought advice from other senators when drafting legislation to solve problems. When he used their advice, they were a part of the legislation and would vote favorably. He had the utmost respect for the Senate, often asking for order when he believed his fellow senators neglected the sanctity of the institution.

On January 6, 1987, Stennis was unanimously elected president pro tempore of the Senate.[3] Senator Robert Byrd commented on his selection, "He is a man who looks like a senator, talks like a senator, acts like a senator, and who is a senator's senator in my judgment. He is well-beloved by all members of this Senate on both sides of the aisle. He is highly respected in and out of the Senate."[4] Stennis was the fourth Mississippian to serve as president pro tempore following James O. Eastland, Pat Harrison, and George Poindexter.

The Senate was his life. He was a good father and husband, but his life centered on his work. It was always with him. His son, John Hampton, commented, "He was a good father, but he was busy."[5] He had little time for relaxation. He preferred to concentrate on the nation's business rather than participate in the plethora of social events in the Capital. He apologized to visiting Mississippians who invited him to social events in Washington, telling them, "My workload in the Senate on matters affecting the people of Mississippi has become so heavy."[6] Occasionally he did manage to find time to enjoy an occasional Washington Senators baseball game or hunting trip to Virginia with his friend Senator A. Willis Robertson and his son, John Hampton.

He often spoke of one memorable South Carolina quail hunt in February 1968, with Robert Jackson and Charlie W. Jones. On the covey rise, Stennis shot three times and claimed he hit all. Jones claimed one of the three. Stennis, not wanting to argue, agreed. However, the dogs retrieved four birds, confirming that he had indeed shot three on the covey rise. Stennis was very proud of killing three quail with three shots, claiming this as one of his best hunts.

Buoyed by his shooting skills, he repeated the same feat a couple of weeks later. He looked forward to dove and perhaps duck and geese hunting later in that winter, maintaining, "This is my only recreation."[7]

According to John Hampton, his father was usually so busy with constituents when in Mississippi, he could only enjoy vacation time in other places.[8]

Whenever possible Stennis would drive his Buick down a pine-tree-lined logging road to a favorite hill on his tree farm near DeKalb. Here he would retreat on Saturday afternoons during football season to hear Jack Cristil announce the Mississippi State football games. According to his daughter, riding the back roads of Kemper County looking at his timber was both relaxing and reinvigorating.

Stennis was chided by his dentist in Meridian, Mississippi for putting off dental work in Washington, due to his heavy workload. The dentist commented, "Had I been there, some committee work would just have been delayed long enough for me to look after my Senator and my friend."[9]

Suggesting that Stennis pay more attention to his health, the attending physician for the Congress of the United States suggested Stennis "get out in the sunshine and fresh air to burn up some of the extra fat in your blood."[10] Other than spending time in the Senate gym and sauna, Stennis found little time to exercise.

Stennis was devoted to the Senate. He expected the same of his staff. Stennis always introduced those who worked for him as "his staff member and friend." He was kind to his staff, but tough. He expected a lot. "You didn't want to disappoint him."[11] His staff arrived early in the office and stayed late, even when they were not as highly paid as other staffers.

Colonel Marvin Rees served on Stennis's staff for two-and-a-half years, from 1980 to 1983. During this time Rees commented, "I never heard him speak meanly or ill of any person. I've worked for a lot of people who have pretty strong egos, who were senators or generals or anything else. And when the pressure would get bad enough, most of them would privately say something cutting, ill, mean or whatever. Never did I hear the Senator ever utter [such a thing]... He might say, 'I think so and so is mistaken in his views... or I feel that he just doesn't have all of the facts.'"[12]

Stennis listed several "attributes" a senator needed: "1. The qualities of basic character; 2. The qualities of a gentleman; 3. Adequate understanding and vision as to the nation's problems in the times in which we live; and 4. A sense of responsibility to the people and to the Senate."[13] Stennis also believed determination, austerity, self-sacrifice, and honor were necessary qualities.[14]

According to a staff member, Stennis took one of three positions on an issue. His first position is based on "his own personal, strongly held convictions …that he will [support] against the majority of voters in Mississippi. Next, how do the majority of voters in Mississippi feel, because a lot of these issues are not 'moral' issues at all. And the third one is basically because a friend needs his help. That's the way the system works, and it should. If it's of no concern to him philosophically, [and] it's not a big deal in Mississippi, why not help a friend out?"[15] Senator Russell Long said of Stennis, "I never heard him raise his voice in conversation to anybody the entire 38 years I've known him. He's always thoughtful and considerate. It's just part of his personality. It isn't just a matter of doing it because the etiquette books say so. That's the way he lives his life."[16]

Actor Charles Laughton chose Stennis as his model for Senator Seabright Cooley in the movie *Advise and Consent* for Stennis "has a charm matched with dignity that combines in a truly striking personality."[17]

According to Columbus attorney Gholson, Stennis was cautious when entering a contentious issue.

> "He was not inclined to assist one constituent in preference to another if they were competing people. If you wanted somebody to really get on your bandwagon and do something for you on an individual basis, Senator James Eastland (D. Mississippi) was much more the kind of fellow to get. He was much more adversarial and less circumspect than Stennis. As far as the Tenn-Tom Waterway is concerned, the most direct person to help when he was inspired to do so was Congressman [Jamie] Whitten, because he had less reluctance to use raw power that any other congressman with whom I dealt."[18]

Whitten once commented about Stennis, "[We] have a lot in common. We're both Mississippians, we're both Presbyterians, we're both Democrats, we both work hard on appropriations, and we're both lawyers by training. The big difference is: I'm a former district attorney who likes to fight for my side, but John's a former judge who still insists on hearing all of the evidence before he makes up his mind."[19]

Integrity

Fellow senators soon recognized that Stennis was an honest, hardworking senator who could be trusted. Throughout his career, his integrity was never questioned. When asked about his actions, Stennis commented that, "I don't want to do anything that would cause me to be concerned with a story in the next day's *Washington Post*." Stennis may have used this answer to placate the reporter, but his moral compass had long been set. John Chancellor, NBC newsman, told the nation in February 1973, "There is not a member of the Senate—liberal or conservative—of either party who would for one moment question the granite integrity of the junior Senator from Mississippi."[20] As a former lawyer, district attorney, and judge, Stennis had tremendous respect for the law and discouraged illegal actions. For his integrity and respect, other senators requested that he write the original Senate Ethics bill as chairman of the Select Committee on Standards and Conduct. This committee was later named the Senate Ethics Committee.

Other senators simply nicknamed it the "Stennis Committee." As chairman he conducted the censure hearings of Connecticut Senator Thomas J. Dodd regarding improper use of campaign contributions. Other senators were so impressed with Stennis's fair treatment of Dodd that they hoped Stennis would be the judge of their improprieties. The journalists covering the hearings named Stennis the "conscience of the United States Senate."[21]

One senator congratulated Stennis, writing, "I want you to know what a magnificent job you did for the United States Senate and for your country in the handling of the Dodd affair. The Senate was very much on the spot, and your willingness to assume responsibility for looking into the matter and making a recommendation on it was eloquent testimony to your great patriotism and your unsurpassed courage."[22] His final press secretary, Rex Buffington, commented on the Senator's integrity, "A lot of that came from being committed to doing the right thing. A lot of his power and influence came not just from the positions he held, but the esteem that people held in him." When Buffington came to work for Stennis, he expected to find someone different from his reputation, but he found the opposite, "He was an individual who was even greater than that wonderful image. It was incredible working for a legend who lived up to and even exceeded his reputation."[23]

Stennis was a "Senator's Senator" according to Frank Sullivan, who served as staff director for both Appropriations and Armed Services during Stennis's tenure. Sullivan recalled that other senators who valued his wisdom would come to Stennis with all types of problems, ranging from personal to political, because they knew he would give them sound advice.[24]

Stennis defended his name when any questions of impropriety appeared. In one instance, Stennis's name was used when the Army removed a lieutenant colonel from duty at Ft. Polk because he complained of inadequate equipment. Stennis had called the base, but did not discuss anything, yet his name was used as a reason for discharge. He directed the Army chief of staff to investigate the matter and "answer this letter, in writing, that you have done your best to ascertain the real facts."[25]

In another incident, a newspaper reported that Stennis and his wife, while on a fact-finding trip overseas, refused to ride on a military plane and called for a special flight to be arranged. When all of the facts were known, the Air Force publicly apologized for its misstatement. Stennis had the utmost faith and respect for the military and would not stand for any blemish on his character that would reduce the military's confidence in him. Stennis did make some early overseas trips with Willis Robertson in which pleasure side trips were mentioned in the plans. However, Massachuesetts' Senator Leverett A. Saltonstall came to Stennis's defense in this instance, "Neither you nor I nor our wives spent government funds unnecessarily, nor did we take any side trips that might be considered for pleasure purposes only."[26] Stennis wanted the military to be well supplied. When he received reports that they were ill-equipped he demanded answers.

Personal Life

John Stennis's Senate life was a mirror of his personal life. He took his Senate duties seriously and was always "on duty." Rex Buffington said that when in public, Stennis could have easily had a sign around his neck which read, "I am here if you need help." During his last term, Buffington recalled that people in airports would approach Stennis in his wheelchair asking for assistance with some problem with the federal government.[27] In keeping with Stennis's sincere desire to help others, he instructed his staff to "show a spirit and an aptitude of being an advocate for our constituents and that we are going to do all within the power of our office to see that justice is done to them. We represent the party in interest and not the Department of the Government."[28] He often told his secretary in the DeKalb office, Bobbie Harbour, to pull out the letters written in pencil on lined notebook paper, because they were "the people who really needed his help."[29]

Many of those who needed help could not come to Washington to seek assistance. In their honor, Stennis kept a "vacant chair morning, noon, and night" in his office to represent "the plain people....They are the ones who really carry most of the burdens in war and peace."[30]

At Home in Dekalb

When people visited in his DeKalb home, his daughter, Margaret Jane, said he would seldom go to the door without putting on his coat and tie. Remaining true to his mother's advice, Stennis was a meticulous dresser. He knew what he liked and would accept few substitutes. Among his favorites was a cashmere worsted suit made in Hong Kong for which he paid $60 plus a $1.50 shipping charge. The owners of the shop from which he purchased the suit also included pictures taken during his last visit to their shop in 1959.[31]

He intended to get all of the use he could from his possessions. When his old briefcase was sent to be repaired, the leather shop could fix a few torn spots, but due to excessive wear could not restore its luster. On their bill, what they left unsaid but implied was that he needed to buy a new one. His briefcase was well worn indeed; every night his staff prepared a "take-home package" of papers that he needed to review before the next day. Stennis always did this "homework" before addressing the Senate or any other group on current issues. Rex Buffington once questioned Stennis's practice of not using the speeches that they had prepared. Stennis told him, "We don't have a problem. You write what you need to write and I'll say what I need to say."[32]

He received so many calls when he was home in DeKalb that he could not get any rest. Before the advent of telephone answering machines, he asked the phone company to install a switch so he could turn off the bell at night. When the equipment was installed he thanked the phone company for their work.[33] Stennis always sent a letter of thanks to anyone who did a favor for him, including notes to his DeKalb neighbors for bringing a dew-berry pie or a few bananas to his house. Stennis had a genuine interest in people.

His records are full of letters he sent recognizing those he met. In one instance Stennis was visiting his sister, Bess, at Baptist Hospital in Jackson. As is customary in the South, when Stennis met someone new, he always wanted to learn a little about them. The parents of one attentive nurse might have been surprised when they received a letter from Stennis congratulating them on their fine daughter.[34]

His own daughter remembers that in her youth when they stopped for gas at a service station, they would sit in the car, while her Dad would learn about the station attendants and their families. He had the same respect for the elevator operators in the Capitol and the waiters in the Senate Dining Room as he did for the other senators. It was impossible to be the last one off an elevator when Stennis was on board.

When visiting military installations, much to the dismay of the generals, he sought out the enlisted men to learn their thoughts. Whereas his actions might be construed as those of an astute politician, Stennis's interest in peo-ple, even those who could do little to enhance his career, transcended politics.

Forester of the Senate

While his standard uniform was coat and tie, he did occasionally put on khakis to walk over his timberlands with his good friend Arthur Nester. He called himself a "pine tree nut." When the seedlings planted on his farm did not survive, he requested the Mississippi Forestry Commission deliver new seedlings during the Senate's Christmas break so "he could personally supervise their planting."[35] His interest in forestry extended well beyond his Kemper County land. Stennis believed that improving Mississippi's abundant forestland's productivity could provide employment and economic growth for his state. In 1959 Stennis was presented the Forest Farmers Association's Forest Farmer of the Year Award for his "outstanding and continuing contributions to the advancement of forestry and full forestry development, not only in the South, but over the Nation."[36]

His colleagues recognized his knowledge of forestry and considered him the Senate "forester."[37]

Stennis met another person very interested in forestry, Dr. Vernon Harper, the assistant chief of the U. S. Forest Service. As a member of the National Forest Reservation Commission, Stennis and other Commission members were responsible for the approval of any lands added to the National Forest System. On a trip to the Institute of Forest Genetics in Placerville, California, in 1953, he saw a bristlecone pine which was over 5,000 years old. Stennis was impressed. Any living thing that was here when Christ was alive was a subject he could discuss with his Sunday School Class in DeKalb. To know more, he contacted the Forest Service's research branch when he returned to Washington. Harper gladly supplied the information Stennis had requested and used the meeting to discuss forestry research.

After visiting a Forest Service laboratory in Mississippi, in the early 1950's Stennis declared that he wanted to replace the nail kegs the scientists were using for seats with modern equipment and furniture. He also knew that Harper wanted to increase the professional level of the research division. Harper wanted more Ph.D.s, but forestry schools did not have the funds to offer graduate assistantships.

Senator Stennis inspects a seed counter at the dedication of the U.S. Forest Service Hardwood Tree Seed Laboratory near the Mississippi State University campus in 1969. According to Dr. Frank Bonner (right), Laboratory Project Leader, when Stennis called the Forest Service office in D.C., the operator would only announce that "The Senator" was on the phone. They all knew which senator was calling. From 1962 to 1970, Stennis supported the construction or renovation of twenty-four Forest Service laboratories throughout the nation.
(Photo courtesy of Frank Bonner)

In 1960, a group of forestry leaders, led by R.H. Westvelt at the University of Missouri, attempted to get additional funds via the Hatch Act, which funded agricultural research at Land Grant institutions. The agricultural community was not willing to share their bounty, so they suggested forestry try for congressional approval of a separate act to secure funding. Given his interest in forestry and his confidence in Harper, Stennis affirmed that he would support any legislation that would improve the level of institutional forestry research. Harper worked with forestry school leaders and the administration to get Congress to act. In the meantime, forestry leaders in various states made their needs known to their congressmen.

In 1961, A.D. Nutting, Director of the School of Forest Resources at the University of Maine approached Maine Representative Clifford McIntire for support of legislation to aid forestry school research. McIntire agreed because forestry was important to Maine's economy. He planned to run for the U.S. Senate in 1964 and hopefully, join Stennis there. The combined efforts of Stennis, McIntire, Harper, and the forestry school leaders successfully saw the Cooperative Forestry Research Act (PL 87-788) through the House and onto the Senate floor. With no time left in the session for a House-Senate conference, the legislation was threatened by several amendments. According to Harper, Stennis saved the day by defeating the amendments. President Kennedy signed the legislation on October 10, 1962. After passage, the act was named the McIntire-Stennis Cooperative Forestry Research Program.[38]

Kennedy agreed with Stennis on the need to improve forestry research. He had even mentioned increasing forestry research in his recent campaign, so he fulfilled one of his promises.

Even though McIntire was defeated in his bid for the senate by incumbent Edmund Muskie, he commented that the McIntire-Stennis legislation was his greatest accomplishment.

Stennis was not pleased with the original appropriation of one million dollars for the program; he had planned for five million. At its ten-year anniversary, Stennis, along with Maine Senator Margaret Chase Smith, was able to add one and one-half million dollars to the budget, allowing the total appropriation to finally get close to the five million dollars he originally wanted. Stennis obtained another notable funding increase at the twenty-fifth anniversary of the act.

He remained a strong supporter of forestry research and was responsible for the construction or improvement of over twenty U. S. Forest Service Laboratories in the 1960s. For these efforts he was named the "Champion of Forestry" in a meeting at Mississippi State University in 1972.

In addition to research, Stennis was interested in helping landowners reforest their idle acres. In 1963 he delivered an address in Union County dedicating the three millionth American Tree Farm acre in Mississippi. Mississippi had then and continues to possess more tree farms than any other state. He spoke at the annual banquet of the Mississippi Forestry Commission on October 20, 1972.

> "I stand before you as a U. S. Senator who has very recently undergone the harrowing experience of trying to get a Forestry Incentives Act enacted by Congress and signed into law. I almost accomplished it. If the House of Representatives and the Executive Branch of the government had been as cooperative as the U. S. Senate, I would have. And I will be back to try again in the next session, and we will get that bill yet."[39]

He was successful the next year with passage of the Forestry Incentives Program. Since trees take a while to become marketable, this program provided cost-shares as an incentive to persuade landowners to plant their unproductive land in trees.

The Stennis Family

Stennis's wife, Coy, was in charge of the house. She provided the senator a meal each evening while they were in Washington. According to staff member Rex Buffington, she was known as "the perfect hostess, and her charm and beauty [were] an immediate attraction to all whom she met."

Presidents, First Ladies, senators, congressmen, cabinet members, and others who make up the official Washington community soon came to know her fondly as Miss Coy. "A luncheon or dinner invitation to the Stennis home was regarded as one of the most cherished invitations one could receive."[40]

Miss Coy was active in local church and school activities, but she mostly shunned politics. Like her husband, however, she was adamantly against corruption in government, and once sent a telegram to Georgia Senator Richard Russell declaring he was not taking a definitive stand on the subject, "[I] urge you make [a] strong statement now, as to your position on corruption in government, all people especially those in the South, need reassurance."[41]

Stennis commented to his cousin Hardy Stennis that the cold Mississippi weather had moved to Washington. For the most part, he took the weather in stride. He had "turned the weather over to Miss Coy when we married and she looks after it and does all of the necessary worrying for the two of us."[42] Having gone through the Depression, Miss Coy was as frugal as her husband. When he ordered a new office constructed in DeKalb, she moved his older office behind their house for storage. In 1978 Miss Coy became ill and returned to Mississippi. She passed away in 1983 and is buried in DeKalb's Pinecrest Cemetery.

Stennis's son, John Hampton, born on March 2, 1935, spent his adult life in Jackson, Mississippi as a lawyer in a partnership with Stennis's friend and former Mississippi Governor, William Winter. Stennis once commented that he had a hard time taking Senator Ted Kennedy seriously because he and John Hampton were both at the University of Virginia at the same time. Prior to law school, John Hampton had been an honor student at Princeton's School of Public and International Affairs.

Later on, like his father, John Hampton served in the Mississippi Legislature. A member of the legislature for fifteen years, he ran for the District 4 U. S. House of Representatives seat in 1978, but was defeated by Republican Jon C. Hinson, an aide to Congressman Thad Cochran. He passed away on September 5, 2013 leaving two children, Martha Laurin Stennis, and Hampton Hines Stennis.

Stennis's daughter, Margaret Jane, born on November 20, 1937, attended Duke University and lived in North and South Carolina just about all of her life. While at Duke, one of her classmates was Elizabeth Hanford, who married Senator Bob Dole and later served as secretary of transportation in the Reagan administration.

Margaret married Samuel Syme, and later Hilburn Womble, both deceased. She has four children, Jane Syme Kenna, Isabelle Womble, John Stennis Syme, and Richard Womble.

Civil Rights

While he never advocated breaking the law or violent actions against blacks, Stennis's stance on civil rights is well documented: he did everything he could to prevent integration. Stennis's son never recalled his father uttering any racial slur. "I have never heard him comment on race as such, as opposed to constitutional issues such as States' Rights and so on, in my entire life."[43]

Remembering the Civil War and Reconstruction, Stennis resented northern interference in what he considered a southern problem, "My idea was that the so-called civil rights bills were too abrupt...went too far and were out of line. Adjustments were made under the law....We finally got out of that extremism. It takes time to make adjustments."[44]

While he accepted the laws requiring equal rights for blacks, he probably never fully accepted the people as social equals. In a letter to Secretary of Defense Charles Wilson, in 1955 he questioned military policy that allowed an expectant white female patient to share a room with two black women, calling the policy "contrary to all the training, rearing and ideals of this young mother and her husband throughout their lives, [and] was naturally regarded as a personal injury and personal abuse."[45]

In a letter to a local supervisor, in 1963 Louie Briggs, he asked that a road leading to the house of their black cook's father be repaired, stating that he "was the right kind of Negro."[46] Soon after the 1954 Supreme Court decision abolishing separate but equal facilities, Stennis submitted the following memo to his files:

> Good relations between the races, painstakingly built up over the years, are deteriorating rapidly in the South under the impact of the Supreme Court decision, the activities of the NAACP, and other outside political activities. As this course continues the toll will doubtless be heavy and the way long. After these outside agitators have run their course, those responsible for this destruction of what good race relations [we have] will retire from the scene of their damage. Then, as theretofore, the patience and understanding of local leaders of each race will again start their painstaking labors and gradually rebuild the understanding and good will between the races. This rebuilding will require years, but it will come— and it will not come through integrated schools.[47]

Race relations in Mississippi did not deteriorate significantly after integration. White academies reduced support for public schools, but the public schools remained. Public schools also integrated their faculties, employing both black and white instructors. In addition, blacks now held public offices in all areas of the state. Prejudices still exist, but the color barrier is not as limiting as it once was. It is poverty and unemployment that continues to hinder Mississippi's potential to improve the standard of living for all its citizens.

In his later years, Stennis hired blacks on his staff and was more open in supporting black initiatives. He recognized that times had changed and that he, along with other white Mississippians, must accept that change. Aaron Henry, former NAACP leader, believed that, "Senator Stennis certainly has developed a metamorphosis over, I would say, the last ten years. I think that much of what happened after [19]82 in terms of support was a true expression of his feelings and, that he had been really uncomfortable with himself in regard to positions he had taken earlier."[48]

In Senator Joe Biden's first meeting with Stennis in 1972, he mentioned that he was elected on a platform of civil rights. Biden was afraid that Stennis, the staunch segregationist, would be offended, but Stennis only commented, "Good, good, good."

As Stennis was preparing to leave Washington in 1988, Eph Cresswell, his chief of staff, encouraged Senator Joe Biden to move into their office. While inspecting the office, Biden found Stennis alone, reflectively gazing out the window.

Stennis asked Biden to sit at the large table in the room, which had a history of its own. Stennis recalled their first meeting and told Biden that the table they were sitting beside was the "Flagship of the Confederacy;" this was where the southern democrats lead by Senator Russell planned their opposition to all civil rights legislation. It was here that the Southern Manifesto was written. Stennis said it was only fitting that the table pass from a man who fought civil rights to one who championed civil rights.

Stennis then commented that the "civil rights movement freed the white man more than it did the black man. It freed my soul."[49] In his later years Stennis realized that blacks had been held back because they did not have the opportunities afforded whites.

Rex Buffington recalled a story Stennis often told about a black friend he had while growing up in DeKalb. Young John asked his mother why his friend could not go to school with him. Over the years as the senator's career flourished, he visited this friend who was not afforded opportunities because he was black. Stennis was also impressed with a black woman who cared for Miss Coy in her later years. Stennis believed this woman had the ability to be much more than a caregiver. She could have become a doctor had she been given the opportunity. Stennis knew that he was partially responsible for holding back black people with his defense of segregation.[50]

He never denied playing a major role in delaying desegregation. At the same time he never advocated violence, and he challenged educators to ensure black schools the same level of education as the white schools. Few educators managed this, though. When Stennis was growing up in Mississippi, the black race was considered second class. This was the culture. Anyone questioning the position of blacks was considered an agitator.

Since black schools were considered inferior, many believed that integration would weaken the educational system. As a result, some Mississippians sought violent means to keep blacks "in their place." Others, like Stennis, sought legal means to maintain the status quo.

From the time President Truman endorsed civil rights legislation in 1948, unitl the Mississippi dual public school system was intergrated in 1970, twenty-two years had passed. By not advocating violence, Stennis may have inadvertently eased the transition and given the white community some hope that integration could be prevented legally, allowing time to adjust to the inevitable.

In his later years, Stennis was more responsive to his black constituents. But in spite of his accomplishments in other areas, he will probably always be remembered as one of the southern senators who attempted to thwart civil rights for minorities.

When asked about his civil rights stand, he often replied he "did not want to go back;" he preferred rather to follow his motto, "Think ahead."

When talk about race became hootless, Stennis changed the subject to advances made by women. He admired Senator Margaret Chase Smith. Her skilled handling of a leadership role in the Senate engendered in Stennis a greater appreciation for the abilities of women to hold public office.

Stennis was of the "old school:" he considered women to be homemakers who remained in the background, but Margaret Chase Smith reversed that thinking. At the end of the 1965 session he wrote, "I could address you as Lady Smith because you are always deserving, regardless of the circumstances, of that true and noble title of Lady Smith in all of the finest traditions of that special title and designation. This is one of the reasons I admire you so greatly and appreciate you so much….You have been a source of strength and an inspiration as I … carry on my own assignments as well as those additional responsibilities which happen to come my way."[51]

Supporter Leo Spatz, owner of the Gilmer Hotel in Columbus, Mississippi, and a Stennis supporter told him, "You are what a man should be."[52] When asked how he wanted to be remembered, Stennis replied, "You couldn't give me a finer compliment than just to say, 'He did his best.' I get satisfaction about doing the best I can, and if that doesn't always turn out well enough, you still have that personal satisfaction."[53]

When the Tennessee Valley Authority and Mississippi State University wanted to put a museum in his DeKalb office depicting his life, Stennis agreed, on the condition that it prove that a boy from a small town can rise to the halls of the Senate. He did not consider himself important. He believed he had been privileged to serve the people of Mississippi.[54]

Stennis recognized that he had been given advantages that most boys in DeKalb and other towns in Mississippi did not have. His family was prominent and considered well-to-do in the community. His brother was a lawyer and his sisters were teachers who encouraged his education. There was never any question he would attend college.

Mississippi Choctaws

Senator Stennis wanted to help the Mississippi Band of Choctaws in nearby Neshoba County. When the senator requested funds for the tribe, Senator Barry Goldwater remarked to Stennis, "It takes more damn money for your Indians than I ever saw."

Stennis and Chief Phillip Martin were good friends. When he and Stennis were talking about the widening of Highway 16 from two to four lanes in DeKalb, Chief Martin jokingly remarked to Stennis, "I would have already done it."[55] During a dedication for a new factory in Kemper County, Stennis was talking about the value of the land and Chief Martin reminded him that it belonged to the Choctaws long before the first white man came to the region. Chief Martin was very successful in improving the welfare of the tribe.

Confidant

Senator Stennis was not as charismatic as other politicians, and he was usually serious. One story goes that if you went to Stennis with a problem he would write down all of the facts and promise to look into the situation. On the other hand, if you went to his counterpart, Senator James Eastland, he would sit back in his chair and discuss crops back home and the weather, and before any business was discussed, he would bring in a staff member to clarify the reason for your visit to Washington. When the discussion ended he would say, "If that doesn't work out, let me know."

Stennis was respected by others because they knew that anything they discussed would be held in confidence. Stennis did not have to talk about or justify his positions. He made his decisions based on facts, and he worked hard to collect those facts. When problems arose in the Senate, his opinions were respected because other senators knew he wanted what was best for the nation.

There were differences of opinion, of course; the Senate was the stage for debate and compromise. Stennis once remarked that it took a stronger man to compromise than would be required to stand on principle. He respected the Senate as an institution. He demanded that others respect it as well when his booming voice called for order.

Early in his Senate career when he was selected to chair the sessions, he did so with little flourish while giving all an opportunity to express their points of view. He held no malice toward others, preferring to agree to disagree. He looked for the good in all, recalling what a friend told him once, "John, there are few five gaited horses."

He strived for perfection, knowing he could not achieve it, reminiscent of Coach Vince Lombardi's admonition to his first Green Bay Packer's team that they seek perfection, knowing they would never reach it, but on the way they would become great. Stennis did become a great statesman. Most Mississippians did not realize the power and respect he had in the Senate. Yet, he did not use that power to bully others toward his way of thinking. He gave members of his committees the freedom to vote their conscience just as he was going to do. He did not seek the spotlight, but preferred to work in the background to solve the nation's problems. He was consulted by presidents for his wisdom. When his ideas were defeated, he accepted the people's will and moved on to the next challenge. He was not vindictive. After the expensive and hard fought campaign with Haley Barbour in 1982, he graciously supported Barbour's cousin for a federal judgeship immediately after the election.

Frugality

Senator Stennis was frugal, to say the least. According to his daughter, "He was a string-saving Presbyterian." In a memo to his staff after the 1982 election, he informed them that while he appreciated their work for the people of Mississippi and the nation, he did not support pay raises based on "the movements of the upward cost of living, whether they have earned it on the merits of their work or not. I just think that this is contrary to human nature and is detrimental to the individual involved as well as the Nation as a whole."[56]

In an attempt to save money, Stennis instructed a staff member to take his Buick to a dealer for service. According to a memo, Stennis had heard about a special service offer on the radio. "Regardless of price," he wrote to his staffer, "Have a special check made to be certain nothing major needs repair, etc. But, of course... take advantage of [any savings] special they are running."[57]

Stennis planned to surprise his wife, Miss Coy, with a new mirror in their DeKalb home. The invoice Stennis received for the mirror was about four dollars higher than agreed, but the mirror was larger. Stennis paid the agreed amount, but made it clear he would pay the additional charge if necessary.[58]

When a piece of country ham that Stennis purchased from a market in Virginia had spoiled, Stennis advised he would visit them later for replacement.[59]

Following his own creed of doing his best, Stennis expected people with whom he dealt to do the same. Asking for no special treatment, he requested invoices from all who worked for him and paid them promptly. When Stennis added a personal note to newsletters that used congressional mailing privileges, he would reimburse the mail account. In spite of the high cost for military systems, which he supported, Stennis always advocated that the country receive "dollar for dollar" for military expenditures.

Stennis believed that generals should be leading the war effort rather than commanding a desk in the Pentagon. As chairman of the Subcommittee on Military Preparedness, his committee set the number of officers. In one instance when the secretary of the Army requested thirty general officers during the Vietnam build-up, the Senator's committee approved only twelve. His tight reign on the number of officers was referred to by colonels who wanted a star as "The Stennis Ceiling."[60] Stennis wanted to be one of the military's best friends, but at the same time … one of their most severe critics.[61]

When budget reductions were necessary, he wanted them spread around so as to cause the government and the economy as few problems as possible.

Stennis was concerned that the Budget Committee was "costing the Senate its committee system which is the Senate's working tool…leaving the floor amendments free to originate and get adopted with no hearings, no record, no analysis and uncertain reasons."[62] Needing to cut the budget, Stennis implored, "We all know that spending less is a requirement. There is no time to lose in getting started. Whose plan is adopted makes no difference to me. What we must have is results."[63] As with other serious issues, Stennis was not concerned with who got the credit as long as results were obtained.

He was as cautious in spending the people's money as he was his own. Material things were not a priority. He had begun his career at the beginning of the Depression. He was a "pay as you go" spender. He believed that running up a huge national debt would impede future generations. He saw what World War II had done to those who remained at home as their loved ones were being sacrificed on the battlefields in foreign lands. He wanted them and the nation to have not only a victory but an end to war. If this was impossible, he would support a strong military as a member and later chairman of the Armed Services Committee. However, he scrutinized their budgets to uncover any waste. A strong military would discourage an enemy from attacking.

He believed that Russia would not support world peace and that other nations would not do their part to combat communist aggression, leaving the United States the world policeman, a role that could not be fulfilled without great sacrifice.

Religion

Stennis was a religious man, but as his friend Ed Brunini Sr. said, "He didn't wear his religion on his sleeve."[64] According to his son, his father held strong religious beliefs, but he was not an active religious type.[65] His moral views sometimes conflicted with the changing times.

When stories turned off color, Stennis would either try to change the subject, or if he could not, he would leave the group. Brought up in a family that believed in Christian values, Stennis never strayed from those teachings. Yet, he never tried to force them on others or allow his religious background to cloud his judgment on political matters. In letters to constituents, in speeches, and addresses to the Senate, Stennis rarely invoked religion. In letters to his church in DeKalb, however, talks in Senate Prayer Breakfasts, and in letters to his family, he expressed his Christian values.

Early in his senatorial career Stennis became concerned with materialist problems facing the nation and world. He longed for spiritual guidance, and joined some of his colleagues in addressing spiritual matters."[66] These meetings eventually evolved into Senate Prayer Breakfasts, which took place every Wednesday morning in the Senate Breakfast Room. Stennis would assign the program and keep a roll book of those attending.

Serving at the height of the Cold War, Stennis worried about how the

Christian community could combat Communism. The rapid rise of Communism in the Soviet Union proved that an ideology could quickly spread if not halted. While he believed in the separation of church and state, he knew that spiritual values upon which his country was founded must be used to combat Communism. He labeled the communists "Anti-God and Anti-Christ."

In a presentation to the Senate Breakfast Group in 1949, Stennis told those attending, "On the world front the Catholic Church and the Pope are the only world-wide unified force[s] to cope with a world front of Communism. Our lukewarm apathetic attitude of secularism …cannot and will not compete with the vigorous, strong anti-God movement of the Communists."[67]

Stennis countered the Communist doctrine by stating, "In a controlled state, everything is offered as free, except freedom and opportunity."[68]

He was also concerned about state support of religion, noting state-isms in England, Germany, and Russia. He wanted the U. S. church to be independent of state support and independent of governmental direction. In his speech,"A Free Church in a Free State," Stennis said, "the church will offer the affirmative spiritual truths, but not serve as policeman."[69]

On a plane trip across the Atlantic in 1960, he visited with the pilot and wondered if he followed the ships at sea to get his direction. The pilot answered that he took his bearings from his instruments and the stars. Stennis correlated the pilot's remarks to his country's challenges. Therefore, he decided that the Constitution, by allowing political, economic and religious freedom, would provide material things. Concurrently, the country would be guided by a higher power for "our bearings and our course."[70]

Surviving A Deadly Assault

Returning from a meeting on January 30, 1973, Stennis was robbed and shot in the chest and thigh with a small caliber pistol in front of his house. The three robbers took his gold watch, Phi Beta Kappa key, and a quarter.

Left for dead, Stennis was able to crawl to the door and call Miss Coy.

When the ambulance arrived, a policeman on the scene directed them to a local hospital. Stennis, however, probably made a life-saving decision when he told them to take him to Walter Reed Army Medical Center instead. There Dr. Robert Muir was contacted, just as he was finishing his shift. Muir had recently returned from Vietnam, where he specialized in treating similar gunshot wounds. He called his assistants, and they stayed through the night. Stennis was told his wounds were serious, but that he could recover.

He recalled a dream in which the newspaper headlines announced he had died in his sleep. He awoke to realize he was still alive and could still be of service. Later, in telling of this ordeal, he said he could hear the doctors talking but could not respond. He wanted to say, "If I can still be useful, then let me live. If not, then let me die."[71]

Later, he would state that a person who had been through what he had must develop a greater sense of service to his country. Able to speak, he wanted to get back to work. He would sneak to a nearby pay phone to give instructions to his staff, when he was supposed to be resting in bed.

On the night he was shot, many of his colleagues rushed to Walter Reed for a report on his condition. President Nixon had his personal physician check with the doctors at Walter Reed, and he visited Stennis as soon as visitors were allowed. Noting that Stennis always had a handshake like a "grip of steel," he told reporters that Stennis's handshake seemed just as firm.

Nixon told Stennis the whole nation was praying for him and that he and the nation needed him to return to the Senate. Nixon told reporters, "He has the will to live in spades.... He represents the nation, not just one region....people may disagree with him, but there is no one who dislikes him. They all love him because he is such a fine man."[72]

Stennis returned to the Senate on September 5, 1973, where all stood and applauded his return. Almost one-half of the Senators gave speeches welcoming him back, citing his moral leadership, courage, honesty, fairness, insight, intelligence, and dedication to the Senate and Nation.

In reply, Stennis thanked them and told them of a letter he received written in pencil from a rural Mississippian, "The writer said that he had heard the news and he said, 'My wife and I did not know what to do. So we decided to go to church. When we got there, we found over half the people in the community already there.' I was overcome with emotion."[73]

Based on a composite sketch of one of the robbers, Stennis's assailants were eventually caught and prosecuted. Two brothers, Tyrone Marshall and John S. Marshall, along with Derrick Holloway, were charged with attempted assassination of a congressman and armed robbery. The assassination law had been passed in 1968 after the assassination of Senator Robert F. Kennedy. The assailants did not know that they were assaulting a U. S. Senator.[74] Stennis never forgave his attackers and objected to their release at pardon hearings.[75]

In the early 1980s Stennis developed cancer. On November 30, 1984, surgeons removed his cancerous left leg. Prior to having his leg removed he was in considerable pain, but refused to use a cane in public. President Reagan visited Stennis while he was recovering, hoping to raise his spirits. Reagan commented that he was the one inspired by Stennis's energy and interest in future opportunities for America.[76]

Believing that a senator should stand when addressing the Senate, Stennis had a handrail placed beside his desk. The desk Stennis used had a colorful history, as it was once occupied by Jefferson Davis. After the Civil War began and Davis became president of the Confederate States, a disgruntled Union soldier struck the desk with his bayonet. The soldier was rebuked for destroying Senate property. Eventually the desk was repaired and returned to service.

Stennis enjoyed telling visitors about his desk and showing them where the bayonet cut was repaired. Traditionally, senators signed the bottom of their desk drawer. Stennis could proudly point to Jefferson Davis' signature, along with his own.

Since Davis was one of Stennis's heroes, he was honored to speak at the dedication of the Jefferson Davis Memorial Park at Fortress Monroe, Virginia, on May 5, 1956. Stennis quoted Jefferson Davis at the dedication:

"I have fought the good fight, I have finished my course, I have kept the faith." It was the way he would want to be remembered as well.[77]

The 1982 election was Stennis's last. According to his former staffer, Steve Grafton, Stennis said, "When it's time not to run, I'll make that decision."[78] He announced in the fall of 1987 that he would not be a candidate for reelection.

Honors

On August 3, 1985, Stennis was honored in DeKalb on his eighty-third birthday. Just about the entire town came to the celebration, where Senate colleagues and state officials praised his record. Throughout his career, Stennis received many honors and awards. He received honorary doctorates from the University of Wyoming and Millsaps College in Jackson, Mississippi. He was a Mason and a member of Phi Beta Kappa, Alpha Zeta, and the Lion's Club.

"The Celebration of a Legend" was held at the end of his Senate career on June 23, 1988, at the Sheraton Hotel in Washington. Senators, Representatives, friends, supporters, and members of the administration were there, including keynote speaker President Ronald Reagan. Telling the crowd that Stennis was an "unwavering advocate of peace through strength," Reagan announced that the newest nuclear aircraft carrier would be named the *USS John C. Stennis* in honor of his service as a member and chairman of the Armed Services Committee.

The "Celebration of a Legend" was sponsored by Jackson businessmen Warren Hood and Robert Hearin with the help of numerous supporters and friends from Washington and Mississippi. The receipts of the $1000 per plate celebration were donated to the John C. Stennis Institute of Government at Mississippi State University. After hearing all of the accolades bestowed on him, when it was his time to speak, he thanked those praising him, but he said the credit for doing what he believed was his duty belonged to his parents and siblings for the guidance they gave him. "They have all passed away, but they were here tonight in part. Some of those good things you've said about me, that's where I got my start, my direction."[79]

In 1989 his birthday was celebrated at Mississippi State University with the dedication of the Stennis Center for Public Service Training and Development. According to his old friend and former staffer, William Winter, "He went out at the top."[80]

CHAPTER VIII
AFTER THE SENATE

John Stennis never lost his love for Mississippi State University. In a letter to a former classmate Stennis revealed that reverence, "More and more I realize and am more conscious of the fact that so very much of my thinking, both on the serious side and the not-so-serious, revolves around experiences, standards, and guidelines established while we were there at the College."[1] He always remained a "cheerleader" for MSU and is considered their most famous alumnus. In 1976 the John C. Stennis Institute of Government was created to "bring about a more effective government through research, training, and service, and to promote greater citizen participation in the political process."[2] This facility is located on the Mississippi State University Campus in the old State College railroad station. From the outside, the station, with its green overhanging roof, appears very much like it did when Stennis and other students boarded the train for home or an out-of-town football game.

His leadership in the Senate left a legacy based on public service.[3] In recognition of Stennis's service to the nation, Congress established the John C. Stennis Center for Public Service in 1988. Located also at Mississippi State University, the Stennis Center strives to bring young people into the public service field by offering leadership training. Congressional staff members from the House and Senate participate in their development programs. The Southern Women in Public Service Conference has featured prominent leaders including Hillary Clinton, Elizabeth Dole, and Geraldine Ferraro. The Center offers a Civil-Military Leadership Program and maintains contact with the *USS Stennis* aircraft carrier.

Not wanting to stop working after leaving the Senate, Stennis gave occasional lectures and had an office in the Mississippi State's Mitchell Memorial Library, which houses his papers in the Stennis Collection. Students interested in public policy were able to discuss current and past issues with him. Stennis loved interacting with the students and was energized by discussing current and past subjects. However, when they asked pointed questions Stennis did not want to answer, he reverted to his tried and true method of talking around the subject without giving a direct answer. He maintained his interest in helping people until his health began to fail. He moved into St. Catherine's Village, a complete life care center run by Catholic nuns, in Madison, Mississippi, where he died on April 23, 1995. His body lay in state in the Old Capitol Museum in Jackson. The only other Mississippian to lie in state there was his friend J.P. Coleman. At his interment in Pinecrest Cemetery in DeKalb, Senate Minority Leader Tom Daschle (D-S.D.), the delegation leader from the Senate, said that Stennis was "a very rare person" who "had much respect from both the Republican side and the Democratic side. He was viewed as a statesman."[4]

In 1975, he was on an inspection trip to his tree farm with County Forester Harold Anderson. Harold recalled that Stennis told him quickly to stop the truck. An old black man following a mule across a red clay hill in Kemper County was probably surprised when a Mississippi Forestry Commission truck passed, then stopped, and backed closer to him. Stennis climbed from the truck, pulled the barbed wires on the fence apart and crawled through wearing his usual pinstriped suit, white shirt, hat, and tie. As he crossed the soft plowed ground the dust covered his well shined shoes. He called to the farmer as he shook his hand and pointed toward the freshly turned soil, "I'm John Stennis, a lawyer from DeKalb. I just wanted to congratulate you on your hard work [plowing with a mule]. You just don't see people working like that any more."[5] His Pinecrest Cemetery marker in DeKalb bears the fitting ending to his trademark 1947 campaign slogan, "He plowed a straight furrow."

FOOTNOTES

Chapter 1

[1] J. C. Warren, Stennis Collection (Later cited as SC), Oral History Interview (Later cited as OHI), August 12/1972, 20.

[2] *Kemper County Messenger,* December 30, 1932, DeKalb, Mississippi

[3] Aaron Briggs, SC, OHI, 2.

[4] Wilmer Daws, SC, OHI, 6.

[5] Ron Harrist, "Stennis formed interest in law, people as Mississippi youth," *Clarion Ledger,* May 6, 1984.

[6] Bobbie Harbour, Interview with Don Thompson, June 12, 2004, Personal files, Golden, MS.

[7] James C. Mott Interview, SC, Pre-Senate Series, 3, 18.

[8] Ibid. 1

[9] Ibid.

[10] Harbour.

[11] Mott, SC, OHI, 2.

[12] Aaron Briggs, SC, OHI, 2.

[13] Geraldus Gay, SC, OHI, 13.

[14] J. E. Hall, SC, OHI, 36.

[15] Turner Catledge. 1971. *My Life and The Times.* New York: Harper and Row. 16.

[16] Mott, SC, OHI, 4.

[17] Gay, SC, OHI, 16.

[18] Mott, SC, OHI, 3, 4.

[19] *Ibid.,* 3.

[20] W. E. Cresswell interview with Don Thompson, June 15, 2004, Submitted to Congressional and Political Research Center, Mississippi State University.

[21] Mott, SC, OHI, 4.

[22] *Reveille*, 1923, SC, Pre-Senate Series.

[23]J.C.Warren, SC, OHI, 1

[24]*Reveille.*

[25]Keith Turnipseed, "DeKalb Native Becomes a Mississippi Legend" *The Reflector*, March 2, 1982, SC, Series 50, Box 41.

[26]*Tribute,* Carl Ruttan C-Span Interview.

[27]John Hampton Stennis, Interview, Don Thompson, December 15, 2003, Jackson, MS, Personal files, Golden, MS.

[28]John C. Stennis (Later cited as JCS) to Theodore G. Bilbo, January 30, 1931, SC, Pre-Senate Series.

[29]Sandra K. Behel, August 1980. *Senator John C. Stennis and the Censure of Senator Joseph R. McCarthy*, Master's Thesis, Mississippi State University, 2-3.

[30]Cresswell Interview.

[31]Warren, SC, OHI, 18.

[32]For a complete account of this trial, see Richard C. Cortner, 1986, *A "Scottsboro" case in Mississippi: The Supreme Court and Brown vs. Mississippi*, Jackson, MS:University Press of Mississippi. In the *Kemper County Messenger* (December 2, 1936) Stennis claimed that the accused were not beaten by any member of the Kemper County Circuit Court. For the court opinions see: *Brown et al. v Mississippi*, 173 Miss. 542 at 559, 572, 574, 579 (1935); *Brown et al. v. Mississippi* U. S. 278 at 285-286 (1936).

[33]*Ibid.*

[34]*Kemper County Messenger*, December 2, 1936.

[35]Democratic Party Newsletter, SC, Pre-Senate Series, July 11, 1935.

[36]Behel, p 2.

[37]JCS, Announcement, SC, Pre-Senate Series.

[38]In Behel thesis from John H. Wigmore, *A Kaleidoscope of Justice: Containing Authentic Accounts of Trial Scenes from All Times and Climes*, Washington Law Book Co. 1941, 473-479.

[39]JCS and J. P. Coleman, SC, OHI, August 22, 1977, 1.

[40]Warren, SC, OHI, 8.

[41]*Mississippi Masters: John C. Stennis: A Senator's Senator*, 1991, Jackson, MS: Mississippi Educational Network, videocassette.

[42]JCS, *Gentlemen of the Jury: A Word to Jurors of the Circuit Court*, SC, Pre-Senate Series.

[43]Harbour.

[44]JCS to Hubert Scrivener, July 19, 1942, SC, Pre Senate Series CF 3

[45]JCS to John McCully, September 18, 1942, SC, Pre Senate Series.

[46]McLemore, Richard A. 1973. A History of Mississippi. University and

College Press of Mississippi: Jackson, MS. Vol. II. pp. 135-136.

[47]JCS to McCully, December 12, 1942.

[48]JCS, *Newsletter*, November 5, 1943, SC, Pre-Senate Series

[49]*Ibid.*

[50]JCS, *On the Beam*, March 31, 1945, SC, Pre-Senate Series.

[51]Wigfall A. Green, 1963, *The Man Bilbo*, Baton Rouge, LA, LSU Press, 111.

[52]Wright to JCS, SC, Pre-Senate Series, January 9, 1947, CF 31

[53]Bilbo to JCS, SC Pre-Senate Series, May 5, 1947, CF 34.

Chapter 2

[1]R.A. Hickman to John C. Stennis (Later cited as JCS), June 24, 1941, Stennis Collection (Later cited as SC), Pre-Senate Series.

[2]W. Butler Gunn to JCS, 1941, SC, Pre-Senate Series.

[3]Frank E. Smith, Stennis Oral History Project (Later cited as OHI) SC, p. 7.

[4]JSC to T.N Gore, February 15, 1947, SC, Pre-Senate Series, CF 32.

[5]JCS to John Hampton Stennis, personal communication, June 6, 1973, p. 1, D.H. Thompson personal files.

[6]Erle Johnston, 1993, *Politics: Mississippi Style, 1911-1979*, Forest, MS: Lake Harbor Publishers, p. 89.

[7]Ibid.

[8]JCS and J. P. Coleman, August 22, 1977, OHI, SC.

[9]*Scott County Times,* in Billy R. Weeks, 1974, The Pledge "To Plow a Straight Furrow:" The 1947 Senatorial Campaign of John C. Stennis, Thesis, Mississippi State University p. 16.

[10]JCS and Coleman.

[11]JCS to John Hampton Stennis, p. 3.

[12]J. E. Hall, OHI, SC, p. 19.

[13]Ibid. p. 28.

[14]*Meridian Star*, August 25, 1947, in Billy R. Weeks, 1974, *The Pledge "To Plow a Straight Furrow:" The 1947 Senatorial Campaign of John C. Stennis*, Thesis, Mississippi State University, p. 12.

[15]*New York Times-Post*, September 15, 1947, in Week's Thesis, p. 38.

[16]S. R. Evans, OHI, SC, p. 7.

[17]Hall, p. 9.

[18]Weeks, p. 25.

[19]JCS to John Hampton Stennis, p. 3.

[20]Wilburn Buckley, OHI, SC, Folder 2.

[21]Hall, p. 5.

[22]Sam Wilhite Interview, OHI, SC.

[23]Weeks p. 28.

[24]Ibid. p. 31

[25]Sam Wilhite, "John C. Stennis: The Gentleman from Mississippi," *Clarion Ledger*, January 8, 1989, SC.

[26]Hall, p. 8.

[27]William Winter, May 21, 1999, OHI, SC, p. 3.

[28]*Webster Progress*, October 30, 1947, 1946-1947, Elections file, SC.

[29]*Webster Progress*, September 4, 1947, MS Department of Archives and History, Jackson, MS.

[30]*Starkville News*, September, 12, 1947 in Weeks thesis, p.14

[31]Robert D. Morrow, Interview, July 23, 1973, in Week's thesis p. 31.

[32]Weeks, p. 35.

[33]*Clarion Ledger* in Week's thesis, September 19, 1947, p. 36.

[34]*Meridian Star*, November 6, 1947, in Week's thesis, p. 41.

[35]Mary Ann Tharp Dazey, 1981, "A Stylistic Study of the Public Addresses of Senator John Stennis," Ph.D. Dissertation, University of Southern Mississippi, p. 158.

[36]James Howell Stennis, August 27, 2005, Interview with Don Thompson, Mississippi Veterans Home, Kosciusko, MS. Personal files.

[37]Hall, p. 17.

[38]JCS to John Hampton Stennis, p. 5.

[39]Weeks, p. 44.

[40]JCS to John E. Rankin, December 19 1949, SC, Series 48, Box 3.

[41]*Tupelo Daily Journal*, October 29, 1947, in Weeks' thesis p. 47.

[42]Weeks, p. 49, 60.

[43]Ibid. p. 53-53.

[44]Morrow interview in Week's thesis, p. 63.

[45]*Jackson Clarion-Ledger*, November 1, 1947, in Weeks' thesis, p. 64.

[46]*Tupelo Daily Journal, Clarion-Ledger*, November 6, 1947, in Weeks' thesis, p. 68.

[47]*Jackson Daily News*, November 11, 1947.

[48]*Webster Progress*, November 6, 1947.

[49]*Time*, Vol. L, November 17, 1947, p. 24.

[50]JCS and Coleman, p. 20.

[51]Frank E. Smith, p. 31.

[52]Senate. Resolution 163, *Congressional Record*, 80th Cong. 1st Sess. Vol 93, Part 8, p. 10569, November 11, 1947.

[53]*Congressional Record*, 80th Cong. 1st Sess. Vol 93, Part 8, p. 10569, November 11, 1947.

[54]JCS and Coleman, p. 23.

Chapter 3

[1]John Hampton Stennis, Stennis Collection (Later cited as SC), Oral History Interview (Later cited as OHI), July 17, 1975.

[2]*Clarion Ledger*, "Stennis friends recall leader's human qualities," Vol. 159, No. 67, April 26, 1995.

[3]Jackson Daily News, November 9, 1947, in SC, subject files.

[4]John Cornelius Stennis, (Later cited as JCS), SC, Series 46, Box 5.

[5]JCS, SC, Series 46, Box 1.

[6]JCS to Dr. Clay Lyle, Letter, Stennis Digital Collection, March 21, 1956, Series 33, Box 3, Folder 074, accessed 5/11/2008.

[7]William S. White, *Citadel, the Story of the U.S. Senate*, New York: Harper and Brothers, 1957, 83.

[8]Gilbert C. Fite, *Richard B. Russell Jr.: Senator from Georgia*, Chapel Hill, NC: University of North Carolina Press, 125-126.

[9]*Widner News*, June 6, 1973, "Sen. Stennis Pays Respects to Russell." Number 11.

[10]Fite, 243.

[11]JCS to Richard Russell, January 30, 1953, SC, Series 28, Box 3.

[12]*Congressional Record*, 81st Cong. 2nd sess. Vol. 96, Part 2, pp. 10671-10672.

[13]Bobbie Harbour, "What Would Stennis Do? Panel Discussion, DVD, October 21, 2010, Jackson, MS, Stennis Institute, Mississippi State University.

[14]JCS to constituent, June 11, 1962, SC, Series 46, Box 7.

[15]JCS, News Release, June 14, 1963, SC. Series 46, Box 7.

[16]JCS to Willis Robertson, August 3, 1951, SC, Series 28, Box 3.

[17]Willis Robertson to JCS, "Suggestions relative to inspection trip October-December 1949," SC, Series 28, Box 3. Robertson was an avid outdoorsman who often invited Stennis to go hunting or fishing with him.

[18]JCS to constituent, January 31, 1948, SC, Series 29, Box 1.

[19]Letter from constituent, November 10, 1947, SC, Series 29, Box 1.

[20]JCS, Letter to constituent, SC, Series 29, Box 1.

[21]JCS, Letter to constituent, April 30, 1948, SC, Series 29, C11.

[22]JCS, Memo, JCS, November 27, 1950, SC, Series 46, Box 1.

[23]JCS, Letter to constituent, January 24, 1948, SC, Series 29, Box 1.

[24]*Congressional Record*, 80th Cong. 2nd sess. Vol. 94, Part 2, 2102-2106.

[25]Bill Keith, "Stennis Warns of Sneak Repeal of Constitution," *Clarion Ledger*, October 23, 1948.

[26]Fife, 246.

[27]Alexander Smith to JCS, Letter, August 2, 1956, SC, Senatorial Correspondence.

[28]JCS, "What You Don't Know About the South," *Colliers*, March 26, 1949, 57-59.

[29]*Jackson Daily News*, "Lynching In South About Eliminated, Stennis Testifies," February 20, 1948, SC.

[30]Fife, 166.

[31]David McCullough, *Truman*, New York, NY: Simon and Schuster, 1992, 588.

[32]Letter from DeKalb soldier to JCS, November 26, 1944, SC, Series 28.

[33]Joe Carrithers, "States Need to Handle Problems," *Columbus Dispatch*, October 26, 1986.

[34]JCS to Governor Hugh White, Letter, February 28, 1952, SC, Senatorial Correspondence.

[35]JCS to Charles J. Bloch, April 5, 1948, SC. Series 28, Box 3. Bloch was a Georgia state representative and an elector at several Democratic National Conventions.

[36]"A Big Man," September 14, 1950, *Webster Progress*.

[37]SC, *Conservation News*, November 24, 1948.

[38]Ibid.

[39]McCullough, 832, 853-854.

[40]*The Washington Times*, "The Senate's Senior Statesman," Insight, February 2, 1987.

[41]Michael S. Downs, 1989, *A Matter of Conscience: John C. Stennis and the Viet Nam War*, Thesis (PhD), Mississippi State University, 14.

[42]*Congressional Record* 81st Cong. 2 nd sess. (4 December 1950), vol 96, pt 12, 16071 in Downs, 15.

[43]Truman, 768.

[44]Downs, 8.

[45]Ibid.

[46]JCS, Memo, The Cold War, SC, Series 46, Box 1.

[47]Downs, 13.

[48]Fife, 358.

[49]JCS Memo, October 14, 1953, SC, Series 46, Box 5.

[50]Cong. Rec. 83rd Cong., 2nd sess. (9 February 1954), vol. 100, pt. 2, 1550-1552.

[51]Downs, 30.

[52]Fife, 358.

[53]Cong. Rec. 83rd Cong., 2nd sess. (6 April 1954), vol. 100, pt. 4, 4671-81.

[54]Downs, 38.

[55]Downs, 39.

[56]JCS, Memo to Staff, June 16, 1953, SC, Series 46, Box 1.

[57]JCS, Memo to Staff, January 23, 1956, SC, Series 46, Box 5.

[58]Richard E. Byrd to JSC, June 20, 1955, SC, Series 46, Box 5.

[59]JCS, Memo, October 11, 1952, SC, Series 46, Box 1.

[60]J.O. Emmerich, "Standing on the Shoulders of Giants," February 1948, reprint from *McComb Enterprise Journal*, SC, Box 1, C-4.

[61]JCS to Eisenhower, SC ,Series 1, Box 1, Folder 27.

[62]JCS, Memo, May 21, 1954, SC, Series 46, Box 1.

[63]Fife, 334.

[64]JCS, Speech, Oktibbeha Citizens Council, Starkville, MS, October 23, 1958, SC, Series 49, Box 5.

[65]Eisenhower to JCS, SC, Series 1, Box 1, Folder 27.

[66]JSC, Speech, Joint Meeting Civic Clubs, Meridian, MS, October 8, 1957. SC, Series 49, Box 4.

[67]JCS, 1956, *Excerpts from a Speech to the Lowndes County Citizens Council*, Columbus, MS. SC, Series 49, Box 5.

[68]Ibid.

[69]JCS to Ed Brunini, April 30, 1956, SC, Series 46, Box 5.

[70]JCS, Memo, February 24, 1950, JCS, SC, Series 46, Box 1.

[71]JCS, Memo, June 6, 1956, SC, Series 46, Box 5.

[72]Idib.

Chapter 4

[1]Bobbie Harbour Interview, June 17, 2004, DeKalb, MS, Don H. Thompson Personal files, Golden, MS.

[2]Steven V. Roberts, "Wisdom in Judgment, 38 Years in the Making," *New York Times*, November 4, 1985, in *Congressional Record*, November 5,

1985. S 14773.

[3]John C. Stennis, A Senator's Senator, Mississippi Masters Video Series, October 31, 1991.

[4]John C. Stennis (Later cited as JCS), Speech, Mississippi State College, October 28, 1957, Stennis Collection (Later cited as SC), Series 49, Box 4.

[5]JCS to James R. Killian, Special Assistant to the President for Science and Technology, December 6, 1957, SC, Series 1, Box 1.

[6]JCS, memo, September 20, 1961, SC, Series 46, Box 1.

[7]JCS, "Final Remarks of Senator John C. Stennis, Dedication of Stennis Space Center," August 3, 1988. SC, Series 46, Box 60.

[8]JCS, Memo, 6/21/62, SC, Series 46, Box 7, Folder 78.

[9]Lester Spell, February 18, 2012, Advisory Committee Meeting Tupelo, MS.

[10]JCS, October 4, 1963, Speech to Mid-Continent Oil, SC, Series 49, Box 10.

[11]Ibid.

[12]JCS, Speech, Greenville, MS, November 1958, SC, Series 49, Box 5.

[13]JCS. Speech, Joint Civic Club Luncheon, Gulfport, MS, November 4, 1958, SC, Series 49, Box 5.

[14]JCS. Memo, January 13, 1969, SC, Series 46, Box 1.

[15]JCS. Newsletter, January 20, 1959, SC, Series 46, Box 1.

[16]JCS, Letter to children and other family members, July 20, 1961, SC, Series 46, Box 5.

[17]"Stennis on Firmness," May 15, 1963, *Commercial Appeal.*

[18]JCS, Newsletter, January 11, 1962, SC, Series 46, Box 7.

[19]Senator Stennis: A Credit to the Senate, *Newsweek* Article, June 25, 1962 in *Congressional Record*, June 20, 1962, S 10299-10300. *New Republic*, vol. 146, Issue 5, January 29, 1962, p. 2.

[20]Stephen D. Young to constituent, January 2, 1965, SC, Series 50, Box 40.

[21]Constituent to Stephen D. Young, January 25, 1965, SC, Series 50, Box 40.

[22]Leverett Saltonstall to JCS, December 15, 1960, SC, Series 28, Box 3.

[23]Chris M. Asch, 2008, *The Senator and the Sharecropper: The Freedom Struggles of James O. Eastland and Fannie Lou Hamer.* New York: New Press, 210-211.

[24]*Meridian Star*, September 16, 1962.

[25]JCS, Memo, January 1961, SC, Series 46, Box 7.

[26]Wroten, Oral History Interview (Later cited as OHI), SC, 22-24.

[27]Mike Espy, "What Would Stennis Do"? Panel Discussion, October 21, 2010, Jackson, MS, DVD, Stennis Institute, Mississippi State University.

[28]JCS to William Winter, letter, December 3, 1960, SC, Series 46, Box 1.

[29]JCS, Memo, December 2, 1954, SC, Series 46, Box 1.

[30]JCS to Ross Barnett, telegram, SC, Series 50, Box 44.

[31]*Clarion Ledger*, September 14, 1962.

[32]For a full account of James Meredith's entrance to the University of Mississippi, see William Doyle, 2001, *An American Insurrection; James Meredith and the Battle of Oxford, Mississippi* 1962, New York, NY: Anchor Books.

[33]Letter to JCS, October 12, 1962, SC, Series 29, Box 5.

[34]Letter to JCS, November 23, 1962. SC, Series 29, Box 5.

[35]James Meredith, "Race Relations Today and Possible Changes for Tomorrow" Address and Comment, February 14, 2008, Northeast Mississippi Community College, Booneville, MS.

[36]J.P. Coleman to William E. Cresswell, March 25, 1963, SC, Series 50, Box 44.

[37]John Hampton Stennis to JCS, September 24, 1963, SC, Series 50, Box 44.

[38]JCS, Memo, SC, Series 50, Box 44.

[39]JCS to Constituent, September 25, 1963, SC, Series 50, Box 44.

[40]Letter to JCS, March 1, 1962, SC, Series 46, Box 7.

[41]JCS, Memo, August 30, 1963, SC, Series 50, box 44.

[42]Erle Johnston, 1993, *Politics: Mississippi Style, 1911-1979*, Forest, MS: Lake Harbor Publishers, 175.

[43]JCS to Constituent, December 16, 1963, SC, Series 50, Box 44.

[44]Marion A. Ellis, 2004, *Dean W. Colvard : Quiet Leader*, Lillington, NC : Edwards Brothers, Inc., 35.

[45]Ray M. Sartor, Interview with Don H. Thompson, June 6, 2005, Ripley, MS, Personal files, Golden MS.

[46]Bill Minor, August 4, 1985, "Stennis' political career survived by small miracles," *The Meridian Star*, 5A.

[47]*Clarion Ledger*, February 12, 1964, SC, Series 50, Box 44.

[48]Johnson, 183.

[49]Michael S. Downs, 1989, *A Matter of Conscience: John C. Stennis and the Viet Nam War*, Thesis (PhD), Mississippi State University, 57-58.

[50]Cong. Rec. 88th Cong, 2nd sess., vol. 110, pt 14, 18133, 18471, 18414.

[51]Pentagon Papers ,Gravel, 3:423; "American Troops Enter the Ground War", Boston, MA: Beacon Press.

[52]Mollenhoff, Clark R., The Pentagon, New York, NY: G.P. Putnam's Sons, 385.

[53]Mollenhoff, 385.

[54]JCS to LBJ, October 28, 1965, SC, Series 1, Box 1.

[55]Downs, 75.

[56]For more information on the Vietnam Senate Hearings see Joseph A. Fry, 2006, Debating Vietnam: Fulbright, Stennis, and Their Hearings, Lanham, MD: Rowman and Littlefield.

[57]*The Clarion Ledger*, November 5, 1967.

[58]JCS to Cyrus R. Vance, August 20, 1966, SC, Series 46, Box 7.

[59]Cong. Rec. 89th Cong, 2nd sess., vol. 112, pt. 20, 26537-41.

[60]Downs, 82.

[61]Cong. Rec. 90th Cong. 2nd sess., vol. 114, pt. 4, 4490.

[62]Dallek, Robert, 1998. *Flawed Giant, Lyndon Johnson and His Times*, 1961-1973, New York, NY: Oxford University Press, 527.

[63]Dallek, 529.

[64]Gay Cook and Ann Adamcewicz, 1972, John C. Stennis; Democratic Senator from Mississippi, Ralph Nader Congress Project, Grossman Publishers: Washington, DC., 14

[65]Ibid, 16.

[66]James K. Batten, November 23, 1969, "Why the Pentagon Pays Homage to John Cornelius Stennis", *New York Times Magazine*, p. 158.

[67]Cook, 18.

[68]Merle Miller, 1980. *Lyndon, An Oral Biography*. New York: G.P. Putnam's and Sons. pp. 367-368.

[69]JCS, Letter, February 19, 1965, SC, Series 50, Box 44.

[70]JCS, Memo, March 3, 1963, SC, Series 46, Box 1.

[71]JCS to Richard Russell, June 22, 1954, SC, Series 28, box 7.

[72]Mike Mansfield to JCS, June 22, 1964, SC, Series 28, Box 7.

[73]JCS, Memo, SC, Series 1, Box 1.

[74]Asch, pp. 243-246.

[75]Bill Minor, October 15, 1987, "Senior statesman goes out at the top," *The Clarion Ledger*.

[76]JCS to LBJ, letter, June 6, 1968, SC, Series 1, Box 1, Folder 29.

Chapter 5

[1]Henry Kissinger, 1968, *White House Years*, Boston, MA: Little Brown and Company, 253.

[2]Michael S. Downs, 1989, *A Matter of Conscience: John C. Stennis and the Viet Nam War*, Thesis (PhD), Mississippi State University, 109.

[3]Aloysius Casey and Patrick Casey, February 2007. "Lavelle, Nixon, and the White House Tapes," *Air Force Magazine*, Vol. 90, No. 2. Operation Menu was the code name for covert actions in Cambodia. The operation is mentioned in Downs, 108-109, and is detailed in Wikipedia, (http://wikipedia.org/wiki?Operation_Menu) accessed on 8/23/2010. See also, David Zucchino, "Fight to vindicate general dies in the Senate," *Los Angles Times*, December 22, 2010.

[4]John C. Stennis, (Later cited as JSC) to President Richard Nixon, March 1969, Stennis Collection (Later cited as SC) Series 46, Box 1.

[5]Joseph Crespino, 2007, *In Search of Another Country; Mississippi and the Conservative Counterrevolution*, Princeton, NJ: Princeton University Press, 184.

[6]Richard Nixon to JCS, August 7, 1969, SC, Series 1, Box 1.

[7]*Ibid*, 175.

[8]Atkins, Joe, "Bork's fate may lie with Stennis," Clarion Ledger, September 20, 1987.

[9]Womble, Margaret Stennis, Comment to Don H. Thompson, December 2, 2014, DeKalb, MS.

[10]Bobbie Harbour, Interview with Don H. Thompson, June 12, 2004, Personal files, Golden, MS.

[11]Stanley Karnow, "CIA in Flux," *New Republic*, January 8, 1973, Vol. 169, Issue 23, 17.

[12]JCS and J. William Fulbright, 1971, *The Role of Congress in Foreign Policy*, Washington, DC: American Enterprise for Public Policy Research, 10, 77. As a part of the Rational Debate Series, Stennis and Fulbright debate legislation limiting the power of the President to enter into executive agreements that could lead to committing troops to a foreign country. Fulbright as chairman of the Foreign Relations Committee suggests stricter limits. Stennis defends the President's ability to act fast, but agrees with Fulbright that Congress should be better informed. Stennis reiterates that Congress can halt funding for undeclared wars, but has never done so.

[13]John Hamner, September 30, 1982, SC, *The Fact Book*, 157.

[14]JCS, Letter, September 16, 1974, SC, Series 1, Box 1.

[15]Gerald R. Ford to JCS, February 21, 1976, SC, Series 1, Box 1.

[16]Ibid, July 19, 1976.

[17]JCS, Memo, December 12, 1954, SC, Series 46, Box 1.

[18]For a complete discussion of the transformation of political power in the South see Joseph Crespino.

[19]Gerald R. Ford to James O. Eastland, President Pro Tempore of the Senate, May 15, 1975, SC, Series 1, Box 1.

[20]JCS Press Release, August 11, 1964, SC, Series 31, Box 24.

[21]Hunter Gholson, SC, Oral History Interview (Later cited as OHI) 10.

[22]"On the Hill," National Taxpayer Union article, SC Series 54, Box 21, June 1981.

[23]Thomas Eagleton, SC, OHI, 4.

[24]Robert Shogan, *Promises to Keep: Carter's First Hundred Days*, New York, Crowell, 1977, 208-210 in M. Glenn Abernathy, et. al., *The Carter Years: The President and Policy Making*, New York, St. Thomas Press, 1906, 180.

[25]Gholson, SC, OHI, 6.

[26]John Hampton Stennis, Interview, February 24, 2007, Jackson, MS. Don H. Thompson, Personal files, Golden, MS.

[27]Center for Oral History and Cultural Heritage, The University of Southern Mississippi, "An Oral History with James C. Simpson," May 11, 1992.

[28]Harbour.

[29]Helen Dewar, "A Gentle Mississippian Plows 40 Year Furrow," *The Washington Post*, December 23, 1986.

[30]Harbour.

[31]JCS to Natchez Trace Parkway Association, SC, December 10, 1947, Series 7, Box 5.

[32]JCS, Letter, June 10, 1954, SC, Series 7, Box 5.

[33]JCS, Press Release, May 10, 1954, SC, Series 7, Box 5.

[34]Jamie L. Whitten to JCS, March 10, 1975, SC, Series 7, Box 5.

[35]JCS to Secretary of the Interior, February 8, 1977. SC, Series 7, Box 5.

Chapter 6

[1]*Ocean Springs Record*, June 10, 1982; *Greenwood Commonwealth*, June 27, 1982; and *Natchez Democrat*, August 18, 1981.

[2]The PAC Manager, October 30, 1981, 3.

[3]Joe Blount, Interview, September 12, 1991, Stennis Collection (Later cited as SC) Oral History Interview (Later cited as OHI) 6.

[4]Rex Buffington, Interview with Don H. Thompson, December 15, 2004, Personal files, Golden, MS.

[5]Blount, SC, OHI, 27.

[6]Haley Barbour, SC, OHI, 36.

[7]Blount, SC, OHI, 10.

[8]Barbour, SC, OHI, 31-32.

[9]*Jackson Daily* News, October 14, 1982.

[10]*Congressional Insight*, December 31, 1981, Volume VI, No. 1.

[11]Weidie, Wayne W. "Frustration hits Barbour campaign," *Ocean Springs Weekly*, October 21, 1982.

[12]Stennis News," October 8, 1982, SC, Series 50, Box 33.

[13]"Battlin Lawyer From Mississippi Battles for 7th Term in U.S. Senate," September 16, 1982, *Wall Street Journal*. .

[14]Buffington Interview.

[15]*The Commercial Appeal*, August 6, 1982.

[16]*Jackson Daily News*, October 27, 1982.

[17]Blount, SC, OHI, 6.

[18]J.P. Coleman to John C. Stennis (Later cited as JCS), October 11, 1982, SC, Series 50, Box 30, Folder C-3.

[19]Blount, SC, OHI, 20.

[20]Barbour, SC, OHI, 35.

[21]*Jackson Daily News*, October 6, 1982.

[22]Kinley Jones, NBC Television Script, SC, Series 50, Box 44.

[23]Barbour, SC, OHI, 30.

[24]Steve Grafton, September 26, 1991, SC, OHI, 22.

[25]Haley Barbour, Testimony, Sub-Committee on Civil and Constitutional Rights House Committee of the Judiciary in Montgomery, Alabama on June 12, 1981,SC, Series 50, Box 40.

[26]James Young, *Commercial Appeal*, August 21, 1982.

[27]*Starkville Daily News,* December 9, 1982.

[28]*Commercial Appeal,* October 18, 1982.

[29]Fred Slabach, July 30, 1991, SC, OHI, 13

[30]Barbour, SC, OHI, 39-40.

[31]Haley Barbour, Comment to Don Thompson, Jackson, MS, October 2003.

[32]Barbour, SC, OHI, 52.

[33]JCS, Memo, December 6, 1982, SC, Series 46, Box 53.

[34]JCS to Steve Grafton, July 25, 1983, SC, Series 46, Box 53.

[35]*Los Angles Times*, April 24, 1995, accessed on September, 26, 2005, from http://thomas.loc.gov.

Chapter 7

[1] Ed Brunini, Stennis Collection (Later cited as SC) Oral History Interview (Later cited as OHI), 48-49.

[2] Leverett Saltonstall, SC, OHI, 19. Saltonstall, a Massachusetts Senator, and Stennis were good friends, corresponding after Saltonstall left the senate.

[3] *Congressional Record*, January 6, 1987, S5.

[4] Gilmer, W, Gerry 1981, "A Fountain of Youth in Mississippi?" Mississippi State University Alumni News, Fall 1981, 10.

[5] John Hampton Stennis, Interview, Don Thompson, 12/16/2003, Jackson, MS.

[6] John C. Stennis (Later cited as JCS), Memo, February 16, 1961, SC.

[7] JCS, Memo, "Once in a Lifetime," SC, Series 46, Box 5.

[8] John Hampton Stennis, Interview.

[9] JCS, Letter, June 26, 1961, SC, Series 46, Box 7.

[10] JCS, Letter August 9, 1956, Series 46, Box 5.

[11] Rex Buffington Interview with Don Thompson, December 15, 2004, Personal Files, Golden, MS.

[12] Marvin Rees, SC, OHI, 34.

[13] JCS Memo, October 2, 1961, SC, Series 46, Box 1.

[14] JCS, Memo, SC, Series 46, Box 1.

[15] Rees, SC, OHI, 38.

[16] The Senate's Senior Statesman, *The Washington Times*, Capital Life, February 7, 1987, 58.

[17] Article, "No Stereotype, Please", *Jacksonville Journal*, August 1, 1961.

[18] Gholson, SC, OHI, 5.

[19] Mary Deibel, "Stennis reaches seniority mark," *The Commercial Appeal*, 1982.

[20] JCS, Biographical Information, Mississippi State University Libraries, 1973.

[21] Charlie Jones, SC, OHI. 5.

[22] George A. Smathers to JCS, July 17, 1967, SC, Series 28, Box 3. Smathers was a Senator from Florida.

[23] Buffington Interview.

[24] Frank Sullivan, "What Would Stennis Do? Panel Discussion, DVD, October 21, 2010, Jackson, MS, Stennis Institute, Mississippi State University.

[25]JCS to General G.H. Decker, March 13, 1962, SC, Series 46, Box 7.

[26]Leverett Saltonstall to JCS, October 3, 1963, SC, Series 28, Box 3.

[27]Buffington Interview.

[28]JCS, Staff memo, April 4, 1957, SC, Series 46, Box 5.

[29]Bobbie Harbour Interview, 6/12/2004, DeKalb, MS, Don Thompson, Personal Files, Golden, MS.

[30]JCS, Memo to Staff, 1950, SC, Series 46, Box 1.

[31]JCS, Letter, October 13, 1959, SC, Series 46, Box 7.

[32]Rex Buffington, "What Would Stennis Do? Panel Discussion, DVD, October 21, 2010, Jackson, MS, Stennis Institute, Mississippi State University.

[33]JCS, Letter, November 21, 1955, Series 46, box 5.

[34]JCS, Letter, November 19, 1956, Series 46, box 5.

[35]JCS, Letter, SC, Series 33, Box 57.

[36]John W. Squires to JCS, January 15, 1959, SC, Series 49, Box 6.

[37]W. E. Cresswell interview with Don Thompson, June 15, 2004, Submitted to Congressional and Political Research Center, Mississippi State University.

[38]For more information on the McIntire-Stennis program see: Don H. Thompson and Steve Bullard, *History and Evaluation of the McIntire-Stennis Cooperative Forestry Research Program.* Forest and Wildlife Research Center, Bulletin FO249, Mississippi State University. 57pp.

[39]JCS, Address, SC, Series 47, Box 71.

[40]Rex Buffington Memos, SC, Series 31, Box 32.

[41]JCS, Memo, July 16, 1952, SC, Series 46, Box 1.

[42]JCS, Letter, March 28, 1955, SC, Series 46, Box 5.

[43]John H. Stennis, SC, OHI, 5.

[44]Joe Atkins, "Stennis reflects on 41 years in Senate," *Clarion Ledger*, October 23, 1988.

[45]JCS to Charles Wilson, September 8, 1955, SC, Series 46, Box 7.

[46]JCS to Louie Briggs, February 16, 1963, SC, Series 46, Box 7.

[47]JCS, Memo, SC, Series 46, Box 5.

[48]Aaron Henry in *John C. Stennis: A Life of Public Service*, 1985, [Video] Communication Arts Co., Jackson, MS: Mississippi Department of Archives and History.

[49]Joe Biden, "Farewell Speech to the Senate," January 15, 2009, accessed from, www.realclearpolitics.com on February 5, 2011.

[50]Rex Buffington, Interview.

[51]JCS to Margaret Chase Smith, October 20, 1965, SC, Series 28, Box 3.

[52]JCS, Letter, November 28, 1955, SC, Series 46, Box 5.

[53]Lawrence C. Knutson, April 18, 1985, *Savannah Morning News*.

[54]Harbour.

[55]Ibid.

[56]JCS, Memo, December 22, 1982, SC, Series 46, Box 53.

[57]JCS Memo, May 17, 1961, SC, Series 46, Box 7.

[58]JCS, Letter, January 9, 1953, SC, Series 46, Box 5.

[59]JCS to Tucker's Market, SC, Series 46, Box 7.

[60]James Batten, November, 3, 1969, "Why the Pentagon Pays Homage to John Cornelius Stennis," *New York Times Magazine*.

[61]JCS, 1956, National Guard Speech, Jackson, MS. SC, Series 49, Box 3.

[62]JCS, Memo, January 30, 1983, SC, Series 46, Box 53.

[63]JCS, Statement, April 25, 1985, SC, Series 46, Box 53.

[64]Brunini, SC, OHI.

[65]John Hampton Stennis Interview with Don Thompson.

[66]JCS, Memo, SC, Series 46, Box 1.

[67]JCS, Memo, August 3, 1949, SC, Series 46, Box 1.

[68]JCS, Memo, SC, Series 46, Box 7.

[69]JCS Memo, July 5, 1949, SC, Series 46, Box 1.

[70]JCS, Memo, Senator's remarks at Presidential Prayer Breakfast, February 18, 1960, SC, Series 46, Box 7.

[71]Harbour.

[72]Nixon, Richard, "Informal Exchange with Reporters After Visiting Senator Stennis at the Walter Reed Army Medical Center," February 7, 1973, Public Papers of Presidents of the United States, Richard Nixon, 1973, General Services Administration, National Archives and Record Service, Office of the Federal Register, United States Printing Office, p. 81. (Google Books, accessed on May 25, 2011)

[73]*Congressional Record*, September 5, 1973, 28471-28477.

[74]*Jet*, March 29, 1973, "Three Young Blacks Held in Shooting of Sen. Stennis," Vol. XLIIV, No. 1, 24. (Google Books, accessed on May 25, 2011)

[75]Cresswell.

[76]Ronald Reagan, in *John C. Stennis: A Life of Public Service*, 1985, [Video] Communication Arts Co., Jackson, MS: Mississippi Department of Archives and History.

[77]JCS, Speech, May 5, 1956, Dedication of Jefferson Davis Memorial Park, Fortress Monroe, VA, SC, Series 49, Box 3, Folder 3.

[78]Grafton, SC, OHI, 38.

[79]"Celebration of a Legend," Program, June 23, 1988, Washington, DC, SC, Program and video available at Mitchell Memorial Library, Mississippi State University.

[80]Bill Minor, "Senior statesman goes out at the top," *Clarion Ledger*, October 25, 1987.

Chapter 8

[1]John C. Stennis, Letter, July 11, 1962, Stennis Collection, Series 46, Box 7.

[2]John C. Stennis, Celebration of a Legend, Washington, DC. Stennis Collection.

[3]Stennis Center for Public Service, http://www.stennis.gov, accessed on July 25, 2010.

[4]Ron Harrist, "Stennis memorialized as 'a great man,'" *The Commercial Appeal*, Vol. 156, No. 117, April 27, 1995.

[5]Harold Anderson, Interview with Don Thompson, October 2003, Personal files, Golden, MS.

ACKNOWLEDGEMENTS

The assistance of those who helped with this project is appreciated. The staff at Mitchell Memorial Library at Mississippi State provided access to Senator Stennis's files. At MSU I would especially like to thank Dr. Michael Ballard, Betty Self, Dr. Craig Piper, Ryan Semmes and Director Frances Coleman.

Stennis's daughter, Margaret Stennis Womble, provided both information and inspiration. She was always a gracious hostess who opened the Kemper County Historical Museum for us.

I would like to thank George Hancock for copying Stennis's pictures at the Kemper County Historical Museum.

I could not have done this without the help and support of my wife, Rita. She read and reread many drafts of this manuscript adding commas and editing my confusing prose.

Finally, I would like to thank Mary Ann Bowen, Governor William Winter and Dr. David Sansing for their reviews of the manuscript as well as Neil White and staff at Nautilus Publishing for publishing this book.

CPSIA information can be obtained at www.ICGtesting.com
Printed in the USA
BVOW08s1734050715

407472BV00002B/75/P